DATE DUE

ADMINISTRATION

AND POLICY-MAKING

IN EDUCATION

administration
and policy-making
in Education

BY JOHN WALTON

BALTIMORE: THE JOHNS HOPKINS PRESS

© 1959 by The Johns Hopkins Press, Baltimore 18, Md.

Distributed in Great Britain by Oxford University Press, London

Printed in the United States of America by Vail-Ballou Press, Inc., Binghamton, N.Y.

Library of Congress Catalog Card Number 59-14896

This book has been brought to publication with the assistance of a grant from The Ford Foundation.

Our stability is but balance, and conduct lies

in masterful administration of the unforeseen.

Robert Bridges, *The Testament of Beauty*

Acknowledgments

A GREAT VARIETY of sources provided the illustrative material that is quoted in this work. In each instance due credit is given the author and the publisher in a footnote, and permission has been given to use these quotations.

Chapter I, "The Nature and Function of Theory," was published in substantially the same form in *Educational Theory*, Volume VII, No. 4 (October, 1957), pp. 240-48. Also, only minor revisions were made in Chapter II, "The Theoretical Study of Educational Administration," which was published under the same title in *The Harvard Educational Review*, Volume XXV, No. 3 (Summer, 1955), pp. 169-78.

The author is deeply indebted to Mrs. Virginia R. Monroe and to Miss Elisabeth Keller for the preparation of the manuscript.

Contents

     INTRODUCTION, 1
  I THE NATURE AND FUNCTION OF THEORY, 5
  II THE THEORETICAL STUDY OF EDUCATIONAL ADMINISTRATION, 21
  III THE ADMINISTRATIVE PROCESS, 37
  IV THE DISCERNMENT OF PURPOSE, 63
  V CO-ORDINATION, 86
  VI PUBLIC RELATIONS, 118
  VII THE SOCIAL ROLE OF EDUCATIONAL ADMINISTRATION, 137
  VIII EDUCATION, 150
  IX ADMINISTRATION AND EDUCATION, 168
  X IMPLICATIONS FOR RESEARCH AND PRACTICE, 184
     INDEX, 201

ADMINISTRATION

AND POLICY-MAKING

IN EDUCATION

Introduction

CONTEMPORARY LIFE is characterized by an ambiguous and pervasive activity called administration, which attaches itself to all organizations. Schools are familiar with it under the name of educational administration. It is not only pervasive; it is also exalted. It consumes the energies of many capable people, and it is considered crucial to the stability and perhaps the progress of the social and political order. Also, it is the object of considerable but diffuse speculation and study.

This inquiry into the nature of administration, particularly as it occurs in educational organizations, attempts to set up a general theoretical framework that will explain with some degree of coherence and consistency the wide range of administrative phenomena. It attempts to define the nature and describe the function of administration, to identify the conditions necessary for its operation, and to make certain assumptions about its relation to other activities with which it is intimately associated. Since the general theory that is presented in the following pages may offer some unusual aspects, it is proper to warn the reader about what he may expect.

The first chapter, entitled "The Nature and Function of Theory," describes several types of intellectual activity that seem to have some relevance for the study of educational administration. However, except for those who may be interested in what the philosophers call metatheory—and they may find the discussion somewhat amateurish—the reader may omit this chapter without serious loss. It has, however, been helpful to the author in justifying the rather wide range of reflective modes of thought that were used in this attempt to formulate a general theory of educational administration.

The following theory is a lineal descendant of the theoretical work of Fayol, Gulick, Urwick, Sears, and others of the school in which administration is clearly distinguished from other activities within an organization. In educational administration this school of thought seems to be on the threshold of a renascence, and it deviates rather sharply from the social, educational, and humanitarian emphases that, for the most part, have tended to diminish the study of administration as administration.

Disconcerting to some readers, perhaps, will be the lack of concern about the psychological and human relations aspects of educational administration. This omission is deliberate. These aspects are the central interest of much of the study that is being done, and there is no indication that it is diminishing. There appears to be some justification for systematic study of the unique characteristics of the administrative process and the structure that it demands.

The reader will observe also that the foundations rest on a few highly controversial propositions. One of these is that administration can be clearly distinguished from the other activities of an organization and that a line of demarcation can be drawn between it and over-all policy-making. A second is that administration is by its very nature incompatible with some of the several intrinsic activities of organization. Whether or not these assumptions will survive empirical or more rigorous logical tests remains a question. Formally, this attempt at a comprehensive theory would have been improved had the purely theoretic and logical components, the hypothetical illustrations, and the alleged empirical evidence been more consistently and clearly separated. However, it is hoped that the distinctions are clear, regardless of the order of their presentation.

In conclusion, the reader should be reminded that this inquiry into the nature of educational administration, which is designed to advance the academic study of the subject, has all the limitations and advantages of a "disinterested" intellectual quest. It has limited immediate significance for the practice of school administration. Ultimately, however, we should expect this kind of intellectual endeavor to contribute enormously to both our theoretical understanding and our practical knowledge of an enterprise on which depends the survival of social organization.

CHAPTER I

the Nature and function of theory

WITHIN THE PAST few years, a lively concern about the lack of basic theory in educational administration has developed. As may have been expected from the beginning, this concern has now begun to turn to the nature and function of theory. Whether this interest in metatheory will divert the energies of students from the more specific problems of developing and testing theories in the field of educational administration remains to be seen; but some attention, at least, should be given to the kinds of intellectual activity that may be regarded as theory. This chapter will serve as an introduction to the methods used in the formulation of the theory that follows.

It should be said at the outset that, considering the current status of educational administration as an intellectual discipline, we shall not confine our discussion to modern scientific theory. Rather we shall look at as many modes of reflective thought as possible, since the progress of our new "science" may depend upon a variety of them. In order to avoid ambiguity in the use of the term "theory," each type may be identified by a descriptive adjective, or the less complicated ones may be considered as components of a more general theorizing process. The difficulty with the latter recommendation is that some of the more elementary types must, for the time being at least, often stand alone.

Types of Theory

If we begin by examining the etymology of the word "theory," not for the sake of discovering its meaning (although we do not have quite the disdain for etymological definitions that many modern students have shown—Pareto, for example), but rather to illustrate one meaning and function, we receive some light on the circumstances of its origin. It comes from the Greek word "Θεωρία," which means a "viewing," a "looking at," "contemplation," or "speculation." In Greek, and in an obsolete English use, the word also meant a "sight" or a "spectacle." [1] Thus, in the beginning, the word referred to both objects and events, and to the primary act of observing. From these original meanings of viewing, contemplating, and speculating, the current definition of theory as a conceptual scheme or system of ideas that is held as an explanation and account of a group of facts or phenomena has developed.

In its original sense theory may have great value for the development of educational administration as a subject of study. If we are ambitious to formulate theories of educational administration that are, or are analogous to, scientific theories, we should be reminded that the origin of the most sophisticated theoretical aspects of modern science lie in the scrutiny of natural occurrences. In the words of an eminent historian of science:

> The beginnings of physical sciences are to be sought in the slow unconscious observation by primitive races of natural oc-

[1] *Oxford English Dictionary* (1933), xi, 278.

currences . . . . The phenomena of the heavens are at once the most striking, the most easily observed, and the most regular of those which are impressed inevitably on the minds of thinking men. Thus it is to astronomy we must look for the first development of scientific ideas.[2]

The question may well arise at this point whether or not the phenomena of the social sciences have been as consistently and as systematically observed as those of the physical sciences. And if so, why has this observation not led to a comparable body of scientific knowledge and techniques? Or are social phenomena less striking, less easily observed, or less regular? All these questions lead to a consideration of the validity of the assumption that the progress of the social sciences will parallel that of the physical sciences; but whether or not they are amenable to the traditional methodologies of the physical sciences, or whether they require a new approach, observation would appear to be a reasonable first step. If educational administration aspires to be a science, it will probably need a Tycho Brahe to precede its Kepler; but if, on the other hand, its data do not lend themselves to the modern scientific approach, observation should reveal some indication of their unique characteristics, including the fact that they may be influenced by the act of observation itself. Therefore, there is a place in the study of educational administration for deliberate observation of the process without any, or at least a minimum of, *a priori* hypotheses of cause and effect relations. As a matter of fact, the study of educational administration exclusively through the testing of hypotheses, however minor, may be premature at this stage of its development.

Closely related to the simple act of observing, which despite its etymological justification can scarcely be referred to as theory, is another type of primitive intellectual activity—that of postulating, or in baroque, behavioristic language, "the coming to react con-

[2] W. C. D. Dampier-Whetham, in the *Encyclopedia Britannica* (14th ed.), xx, 115–16.

sistently to an entity, which is, in reality, a segment of a chaotic flux of stimuli." The psychologist Edwin G. Boring has pushed this type of theorizing back beyond the mind of man:

> Surely before man animals had scientific theories, generalizations about variable nature. Here I am suggesting, with the contributions of Gestalt psychology in mind, that an object is a theory about an invariance in ever changing and chaotic experience. Since size constancy has been found for chickens and apes, it is plain that they know how to make the basic classifications of objects as to size, that they act in accordance with a theory of the invariance of the objective size.[3]

This definition of theory extends it to subhuman minds and to the instant when objects or events are identified, distinguished from other objects and events or from the indeterminate flux of experience, and given some rudimentary kind of conceptual status. The distinguishing feature of the object in the illustration given above was invariance in size, but the theory might have postulated any one of a number of other characteristics by which the object might have been identified. Although it may be extremely farfetched to compare such theorizing of chickens and apes about the size constancy of objects as a means of identifying them to the attempts of the human mind to identify the processes and events of administration in the chaotic world of human experience, the analogy may have some value. The current emphasis on theory as an intellectual activity concerned with relationships between concepts, and the relaxation of philosophical tension in the matter of definition may have obscured the value of this more primitive type of theorizing for the study of subjects consisting of variable and ill-defined phenomena. The study of educational administration, therefore, may be advanced by the type of theorizing that postulates particular events in such a way that they can be identified.

What we are saying is that the intellectual activity that identifies

[3] Edwin G. Boring, "The Role of Theory in Experimental Psychology," *The American Journal of Psychology*, LXVI (April, 1953), 175.

The Nature and Function of Theory

phenomena—objects, events, or sets of conditions—is a type of theorizing. Its function is that of distinguishing some object, event, or combination of events and objects from other phenomena, or at a very elementary level, from an undifferentiated continuum of experience. This procedure has many stages. Rarely do we identify a phenomenon *de novo*. Most phenomena with which we deal already enjoy some public identification, and the problem often consists of making the identification more precise.

From identification we proceed to definition, although there may be serious disagreement here as to the temporal relation. If this identification is to enter into the community of discourse and into the realm of logical relations, it must be defined. Presumably this has been the order of development in the physical sciences.

> A physical theory starts with primitive, unrefined concepts, such as the notions of space and time. It proceeds to the construction of more precisely defined constructs, for instance, mass and force in mechanics, into whose definition there enter both epistemic (operational) and constitutive (theoretical) characteristics. The next step is the postulation of relationships connecting the constructs (for example, the principles of mechanics, like $F = ma$). Next in order are logical deductions by appropriate mathematical manipulation of relationships between quantities all of which have sufficient epistemic significance to be measurable in the laboratory. If these relationships are sufficiently general in character, they are called physical laws . . . , that is, they are supposed to describe adequately routines or patterns of physical experience.[4]

A definition, although based on the assumption that there is some kind of correspondence between the concept and a "real" entity, does not have the primary function of demonstrating this correspondence. Rather, it attempts to refine the concepts so that they may be used as unambiguously as possible. The current definitions of educational administration tend to be vague and ambiguous; through imagination, speculation, and analysis they

[4] R. B. Lindsay, "Operationalism in Physics," in *The Validation of Scientific Theories*, Philipp G. Frank, ed. (Boston: Beacon Press, 1957), pp. 70–71.

may become more precise and, therefore, more easily distinguished from and linked with other concepts and terms.

Since "operational" definitions enjoy tremendous prestige today, not only in the natural but also in the social sciences, we shall note briefly their special characteristics. Bridgman has explained this mode of definition as follows:

> A term is defined when the conditions are stated under which I may use the term and when I may infer from the use of the term by my neighbor that the same conditions prevailed.[5]

Again:

> The fundamental idea back of an operational analysis is . . . that we do not know the meaning of a concept unless we can specify the operations which were used by us, or by our neighbor in applying the concept in any concrete situation.[6]

In spite of the apparent simplicity of Bridgman's idea, operationalism has been variously construed.[7] However, in its simplest form it remains quite clear and straightforward. If an operationalist attempted to define the commonplace notion of length, he would probably take as his definiendum, not the single term "length," but a whole sentence, say in this instance, "The length of this desk is five feet." He would then define this statement by saying that if one lays off the top of the desk in a certain manner with a foot rule, one will observe the coincidence of the corner of the desk with the end of the foot rule at the fifth step. The ontological question "What is length?" is completely avoided. But operationalism has not been restricted to instrumental situations, and the question has arisen as to how far this procedure may be extended

[5] P. W. Bridgman, "Some General Principles of Operational Analysis," *Psychological Review*, LII (September, 1945), 246; see also his *Logic of Modern Physics* (New York: The Macmillan Company, 1927).

[6] Bridgman. "The Nature of Some of our Physical Concepts," *British Journal for the Philosophy of Science*, 1 (February, 1951), 257.

[7] See, for example, Philipp G. Frank, ed., *The Validation of Scientific Theories*, Chap. II.

The Nature and Function of Theory

to include pencil-and-paper conditions without losing all distinctiveness as a special kind of definition.

Perhaps we may apply the original and simplest form of operational definition to administration as follows: "If a person is placed in charge of a school or school system, that is, he assumes an 'administrative position,' he employs staff, prepares budgets, directs the activities of people in their reciprocal relations, checks results, etc." These operations, it will be noted, are described by a vocabulary that probably is more familiar, or at least less ambiguous, than the word we are defining, otherwise there would be no gain in the clarity of definition.

It would be unwise to try to read too much into operationalism as theory or to expect very much from it in the way of a contribution to theory-making. Bridgman apparently believed that a concept was synonymous with a set of operations, but it is difficult to determine what the term "operations" includes. He did not expect operationalism to limit or to exclude what we have called theoretical definitions. "In general," he said, "I think that there need be no qualms that the operational point of view will ever place the slightest restriction on the freedom of the theoretical physicist to explore the consequences of any free mental construction that he is ingenious enough to make." [8]

Numerous attempts have been made to define administration. Although there seems to be substantial agreement among the definitions, much remains to be done in making them clear and unambiguous. A few examples from both public and educational administration will show the current status of definition in the field:

> When two men co-operate to roll a stone that neither could have moved alone, the rudiments of administration have appeared.[9]

[8] P. W. Bridgman, "The Present State of Operationalism," in *The Validation of Scientific Theories*, p. 79.
[9] Herbert A. Simon, Donald Smithburg, and Victor A. Thompson, *Public Administration* (New York: The Macmillan Company, 1950), p. 3.

Administration has to do with getting things done; with the accomplishment of defined objectives. The science of administration is thus the system of knowledge whereby man may understand relationships, predict results, and influence outcomes in any situation where men are organized at work together for a common purpose.[10]

Administration is the capacity to co-ordinate many, and often conflicting, social energies in a single organism, so adroitly that they shall operate as a unity.[11]

... school administration may be defined as the selection, appointment, and assignment of the school's employed personnel, and the coordination and leadership of all school-associated personnel-employees, pupils, board members, and members of the community—in creating, executing, and improving policies which make for sound and efficient education. Personnel—its procurement, coordination, and leadership—is one main element in this definition. Policies—their creation, implementation, and improvement—comprise another. Achievement of sound educational goals is the third.[12]

In common usage, the term administration is roughly synonymous with that of management. In its proper use in education, it means much that we mean by the word government and is closely related in content to such words as superintendence, supervision, planning, oversight, direction, organization, control, guidance, and regulation. Besides referring to the process or activity of managing people and materials, the term is regularly used to designate the person or persons, the officials, in charge of the activity.[13]

... administration [is] a hierarchy of subordinate-superordinate relationships within an institution. In this relationship three di-

[10] Luther H. Gulick and L. Urwick, eds., *Papers on the Science of Administration* (New York: Institute of Public Administration, Columbia University, 1937), p. 191.

[11] Brooks Adams, *The Theory of Social Revolution* (New York: The Macmillan Company, 1913), pp. 207–208.

[12] Benjamin Floyd Pittenger, *Local Public School Administration* (New York: McGraw-Hill Book Company, 1951), p. 7.

[13] Jesse B. Sears, *The Nature of the Administrative Process* (New York: McGraw-Hill Book Company, 1950), p. 4.

The Nature and Function of Theory

mensions are of critical importance: (a) The authority dimension, that is, the source of the superordinate's dominance and the subordinate's acceptance of it. . . . (b) The scope dimension, that is, the range of the roles and facilities legitimately included within the interaction. These must be functionally specific rather than functionally diffuse. (c) The affectivity dimension, that is, the distinctive character of the personal relationship.[14]

From even a cursory review of the above definitions two facts are apparent: (1) there seem to be some common elements in most, if not all, of them; and (2) the study of administration would profit from more precisely formulated definitions.

Following immediately upon definition is systematic classification, in which constructs are used for the identification and ordering of data that are observed. Thus a definition of administration would provide a means of classifying certain observable events as administration. As a matter of fact we are able now to do this to some extent, but there are borderland areas in administration that constitute a difficult realm for the student. Policy-making for instance, also often vaguely defined, is sometimes classified as administration, sometimes not. The ambiguous definitions that we have often are of little help. If the definition could be made more precise, we should be able to recognize and to classify certain phenomena as administration whenever we see them and to use the definition more precisely in its subsequent relations.

Analytical theory is another approach to the study of administration that has been useful. The breaking down of a whole into its parts has been a fruitful activity in chemistry and psychology, and it marks the beginning of the systematic study of education. In psychology, the analysis of personality into traits, needs, and abilities [15] and the analysis of mind by the mathematical treatment

[14] Francis S. Chase and Egon G. Guba, "Administrative Roles and Behavior," *Review of Educational Research*, xxv, No. 4 (October, 1955), 282. Quoted from Arthur P. Coladarci and Jacob W. Getzels, *The Use of Theory in Educational Administration* (Palo Alto, Calif.: Stanford U. Press, 1955).
[15] See R. B. Cattell, *Description and Measurement of Personality* (Yonkers-on-Hudson: World Book Company, 1946), p. 4.

of experimental data obtained from intelligence tests [16] have been important procedures in the development of advanced study.

The classic examples of the study of administration by this method are Henri Fayol's attempt to analyze the phenomenon into its separate functions [17] and Luther H. Gulick's extension of this analysis, the now familiar POSDCORB.[18] In educational administration similar analyses have been made by Sears,[19] Hagman and Schwartz,[20] and Chase.[21]

The limitations of classification and analysis have been stressed frequently and recently in the literature on administration. Halpin, while realizing their importance, insists that they be carefully distinguished from "genuine" theories, and he proceeds to point out the hazards in preoccupation with taxonomies such as excessive verbalism and the mixing of different levels of categories.[22] His admonitions should be heeded; nevertheless there is no gainsaying that classification and analysis are a kind of theorizing and that they are important, with all their limitations, in the development of more advanced theories.

The next type of theory that we shall discuss may be called simple empirical correlation. In theories of this type relationships are assumed without attempting to control all the variables. As scientific theories, they are naive and often misleading. For example, we may find that school superintendents with doctor's degrees are more successful than those who do not possess such

[16] See Godfrey H. Thomson, *The Factorial Analysis of Human Ability* (Boston: Houghton Mifflin Company, 1939).

[17] Henri Fayol, *Industrial and General Administration*, English translation by J. A. Coubrough (Geneva: International Management Association, 1930).

[18] "Notes on the Theory of Organization," in *Papers on the Science of Administration*.

[19] Jesse B. Sears, *The Nature of Administrative Process* (New York: McGraw-Hill Book Company, 1950).

[20] Harlan L. Hagman and Alfred Schwartz, *Administration in Profile for School Executives* (New York: Harper & Brothers, 1955).

[21] Francis S. Chase, "New Program in Administration," *The Elementary School Journal*, February, 1955, p. 311.

[22] Andrew W. Halpin, *Administrative Theory in Education* (Chicago: Midwest Administration Center, University of Chicago, 1958), pp. 7-9.

degrees. We might logically assume then that by selecting a superintendent with a doctor's degree, the probabilities are that we shall get a better superintendent than if we had selected one with only a bachelor's degree. However, we could not assume that it is the doctor's degree that causes the superintendent to be more successful than his less academically persistent colleague. Although such an assumption is often made, the possession of a doctor's degree may merely be an index to certain qualities that make for successful administration, and as such it may have predictive value in the selection of superintendents, but it does not necessarily presuppose cause and effect relationship.

The type of intellectual activity most congenial to science is explanatory theory. The form that explanatory theory invariably takes is: Let Q be the thing to be explained (the explicandum); then an explanation of Q will take the following form: because of P; and if P, then Q.[23] Restating this theory in terms with referents we may get: Because teachers receive annual increments in salary, their satisfaction in teaching will be higher than if they do not receive these increments. This theory states explicitly that satisfaction in teaching is increased by salary increments, and this is something quite different from saying that where a policy of annual increments is in effect, teacher satisfaction is higher than where such a policy does not exist. In the latter statement annual salary increments are said to be found in company with high teacher satisfaction; in the former they are said to be at least one thing that will bring about, i.e. "cause" an increase in, teacher satisfaction.

We should note here that as we attempt to explain why some teachers enjoy greater satisfactions than others, we are not dealing directly with empirical facts, but with generalizations about relationships between concepts. It may well be that increased

[23] See C. J. Ducasse, "The Nature and Function of Theory" *Ethics*, LI (October, 1940), 26. Although he divides such theories into two classes, "causal" and "conceptual," both presuppose a kind of causality. Therefore we shall classify all such theories as explanatory or causal, whether the terms refer to empirical events or are merely constructs with logical relations.

salaries are, as are most things in daily life, empirical facts. But when we begin to theorize, we are dealing with the concepts of "teacher," "salary," "increments," and "satisfaction," which presumably correspond to empirical objects or occurrences. However glibly we employ these concepts, they contain two obscure elements; the definitions that should accompany the concepts, and the method prescribed for deciding what empirical entities shall be regarded as exemplifying the concepts. Since they have become so familiar, we are likely to overlook the fact that at one time the objects or phenomena that they represent were abstracted from experience and differentiated from all other phenomena by types of theorizing that we have called definition and classification. Not only do these concepts presumably have "real" or empirical referents, but it can also be demonstrated that they are related to one another in various ways. They do, however, exhibit different degrees of ambiguity.

In addition to concepts that refer to comparatively unambiguous empirical events, theory employs constructs, often in the form of intervening variables, as designata for postulated phenomena that are not observable. One psychologist has questioned the necessity for hypothetical constructs and intervening variables,[24] but many of his colleagues employ them; and in the study of educational administration, theory will be concerned with both concepts that have empirical referents of varying degrees of unambiguity and hypothetical constructs. For example, it is an oft-repeated theory that the concentration of authority increases efficiency of operation in organizations. Here the concepts are "concentration," "authority," "increase," and "efficiency." Obviously, "authority" and "efficiency" are liable to a high degree of ambiguity, and the credentials for the admission of empirical entities into these concepts are not closely specified as are those for the referents of the concepts "teacher" and "salary increment." To illustrate how we may use an intervening variable, we may say

[24] See B. F. Skinner, "Are Theories of Learning Necessary," *Psychological Review*, LVII (July, 1950), 193–216.

The Nature and Function of Theory

that "faculty participation in policy-making" produces "co-operative teachers." Now the concepts used here are reasonably easy to define in concrete terms; but we may postulate an intervening variable such as "self-respect" or "morale" to explain why participation in policy-making increases co-operation. Furthermore, this intervening variable may be employed to explain a wide range of phenomena. It is with the causal relationships between concepts ranging the whole continuum of abstraction that explanatory theory deals.

Modern scientific theories often integrate some of the different kinds of theorizing into what is called a hypothetico-deductive system in which the terms are expressed mathematically; and some metatheorists have suggested that the word theory should be limited to systems of this kind:

> In order to provide for a terminology which will not constantly involve us in a tangle of confusions, I propose to define "theory" as a set of assumptions from which can be devised by purely logico-mathematical procedures a larger set of empirical laws. The theory thereby furnishes an explanation of these empirical laws and unifies the originally relatively heterogeneous areas of subject matter characterized by those empirical laws. Even though it must be admitted that there is no sharp line of demarcation (except a purely arbitrary one) between theoretical assumptions and empirical laws the distinction at least in the sense of a gradation, is illumination from a methodological point of view.[25]

In establishing the criteria of a good theoretical system, some students have looked to Newton's *Principia* as a model. Hull, for example, summarized the criteria for a good theory somewhat as follows:

> The definitions and postulates, which correspond to axioms in mathematics, should be consistent with one another. Deductions, which constitute the substance of the system, should be rigorously drawn and clearly explained step by step. The theo-

[25] Herbert Feigl, "Principles and Problems of Theory Construction in Psychology" in *Current Trends in Psychological Theory* (Pittsburgh: University of Pittsburgh Press, 1951), p. 182.

rems that are so deduced should take the form of specific statements about the outcome of concrete experiments or observations. And finally the untested statements should be verified or discredited by empirical evidence.[26]

Now it may not be technically possible to test the theorems so deduced, although empirical tests are conceivable. While thoroughgoing empiricists would probably be impatient with situations of this kind, it would seem that the importance of a theory as theory would not depend upon the accidents of technical possibilities.

The difficulties in constructing a hypothetico-deductive theoretical system for educational administration are apparent. With what axioms, mutually consistent and expressed in unambiguous or mathemtical terms, would it begin? Generally, the statements that can be made about organizations, human behavior, group behavior, and the nature of administration and education, which may serve as basic postulates, lack clearness and precision and often they are not productive of deductions, either because of an inherent barrenness or because of their obscurity. Nevertheless, however premature hypothetic-deductive theories may be in educational administration at this time, we can never be sure when a set of postulates will yield under rigorous deductions highly important hypotheses. Therefore, efforts in this direction should be encouraged.

Range of Theory

The range of theory has two dimensions. As has been shown in the discussion up to now, it can extend from the identification and classification of phenomena to a hypothetico-deductive system

---

[26] Clark L. Hull, "Hypothetico-Deductive Method of Theory Construction," in Lawrence M. Stolurow's *Readings in Learning* (New York: Prentice-Hall, Inc., 1953), pp. 9–30.

that relates and explains a hitherto heterogeneous mass of data and produces new data. All these intellectual activities have been classified as theorizing because they are all reflective on experience, all deal with concepts, and all are in some degree tentative, although they may be expressed in the strongest declarations. Also, there is an interdependence among them.

The second dimension is the extent of application on the basis of which we may divide theories into four classes. First, there is the minor working hypothesis, one step removed from naive empiricism. For example, a school superintendent may "theorize" that if class size is reduced, Johnny will learn to read better, and he may put Johnny in a smaller class, with or without checking the results. Second, there are theories of the middle range that attempt to explain a class of phenomena. For example, the hypothesis given above may be raised to include all learning and may take some such form as: Learning depends on the personal relationship between teacher and student. Third, there is the single, simple, grand theory that attempts to explain all human behavior, whether in organizations or out of them. Thus Freud might explain administrative behavior in the same way that would explain all other behavior; or Toynbee might invoke his thesis of "challenge" and "response." Finally, there can be a general conceptual scheme that relates theories of the middle and lower ranges into a system of logically consistent propositions, which does not necessarily or immediately aspire to a single explanation, but aims to provide a kind of conceptual framework for the field of study.

Rather curious is the fact that so much intellectual activity has been characterized by a quest not only for predictability but also for simplicity and unity. As a matter of fact the prestige of a theory varies directly with the reduction of the number of explanations for an increasing range of phenomena—*simplex sigillum veri*. At the working level perhaps simplicity is preferred to unity, but the hope seems implicit in the assumptions of scientific searchers that all endeavors will lead ultimately to one grand principle that will explain all phenomena. A history of theory might reveal differences in this emphasis at different times—between Moses and Aristotle, for example—but the intellectual heroes of the modern world are monists.

Limitations of Theory

A theory can never express a preference or an imperative. Since educational administration is suffused with values and highly dependent upon directives for its operation, skepticism about the value of theory by practicing administrators may be justified by the nature of their task. In the acts of deciding what should be done, or of accepting the decisions of others about what should be done, and in issuing directives to the organization, the administrator abandons theory. Decisions about what is right and good and desirable, and how the objectives may be obtained, must be positive, clear, and imperative. The speculative tentativeness of theory, while ultimately of great value to effective administration, may well appear to be a hindrance.

So far the contributions of theory to the role of values in administration have been limited and indirect. Obviously, definition, classification, and analysis can contribute to the clarification of values and objectives, and explanatory theory may help us understand why certain values are held. For example, the value of efficiency in education, i.e., achieving the maximum results with the least expenditure of time, energy, and money, may reflect the prevalence of a certain school of economic thought. Also, explanatory theory may help us ascertain what procedure will be most likely to achieve the results that are valuable. However, theory has contributed little to our understanding why some values should be preferred to others. If we follow the labyrinth of the relations between fact and value to the end, the last turn leaves us facing a wall of pure preference or prescription.

CHAPTER II

the Theoretical study of educational administration

THE EXISTENCE OF administrative phenomena is clearly established, but their characteristics, relations, and laws are obscure. This condition—the knowledge of the existence of a phenomenon without a clear understanding of it or without even an unambiguous definition—is typical of the state of much of our knowledge. Fewer and less precise concepts are necessary for the recognition and crude manipulation of phenomena than for the understanding of their fundamental nature, relations, and limitations. Our understanding follows painfully and slowly behind our ability to identify and to manipulate. The fact that this condition is more pronounced in the social than in the physical sciences accounts for the impatience and bewilderment of the exact scientist in the study of the more ambiguous social phenomena. The reasons for the difference are of no major concern here; we wish merely to call attention to the fact that the object of our study belongs in the category of those phenomena that are generally recognized, often successfully but imprecisely manipulated, and only very vaguely understood.

Consequently, the subject matter of educational administration is not a thing of intellectual beauty. Borrowing fragments from several diverse and comparatively advanced fields of study—law, political science, social psychology, sociology, ethics, economics, business, engineering, architecture, and statistics—it lacks an organized body of subject matter of its own. It possesses no simple and elegant theoretical structure; it can present no series of well-established empirical relations; and it lacks an ordered record of events. In addition to the fragments appropriated from other fields of study, the content of the courses in educational administration has consisted of a description of practices, the cautious recommendation of promising techniques, and personal success stories and lively anecdotes, all surrounded with the aura of common sense, and often purveyed with both lively good humor and appropriate soberness. Helpful as this pedagogical method is to the prospective or practicing administrator, it has not contributed a great deal to the development of the subject as an academic discipline with all that phrase implies.

The current interest in the theoretical aspects of educational administration indicates a dissatisfaction with the traditional study of the subject, as well as a desire to formulate a rubric of administrative doctrine or a comprehensive theoretical framework. The latter, if and when it is formulated, should account for many, if not all, aspects of educational administration—its nature and function, origin and growth, internal and external relations, limitations and powers—and thus transcend and encompass the conventional ideas of administrative theory, e.g., "The theory of administration is concerned with how an organization should be constructed and operated in order to accomplish its work effectively." [1] Such a theory, provided that it were free from internal contradictions, would furnish a structure for the inchoate mass of

---

[1] Herbert A. Simon, *Administrative Behavior* (New York: The Macmillan Company, 1955), p. 38. See, also, Arthur P. Coladarci and Jacob W. Getzels, *The Use of Theory in Educational Administration*, Educational Administration Monographs, No. 5 (Palo Alto, Calif.: Stanford University Press, 1955), pp. 15–27.

The Theoretical Study of Educational Administration

data and opinion that characterizes the field at the present time. Also, it would account for the empirical relations that have been observed, and it would permit deductions that could be expressed in the form of verifiable hypotheses.

Whether such a comprehensive theory can be constructed at this time out of the odds and ends of empirical data is debatable. Perhaps less ambitious and grandiose attempts to construct more limited theories of relationships would be more fruitful. However, Merton, in his work on social theory, recommends that both types of theorizing be carried on:

> For to concentrate entirely on special theories is to run the risk of emerging with unconnected ad hoc speculations consistent with a limited range of observations and inconsistent among themselves.

While

> To concentrate entirely on the master conceptual scheme for deriving all subsidiary theories is to run the risk of producing twentieth-century sociological equivalents of the large philosophical systems of the past, with all their varied suggestiveness, all their architectonic splendor and all their scientific sterility.[2]

Realizing that any master conceptual scheme at this time must be rather loosely drawn, we propose to attempt one, which at the least should be fruitful as a source of testable theories of a lower range.

It is well to begin with a consideration of the achievements of our predecessors. Interest in the subject has not been lacking. In 1916 Cubberley was bold enough to present in systematic fashion some of the fundamental principles that he thought would provide the practitioner of educational administration a guide for "proper action." A combination of factual statements, normative judgments, and prudential maxims, this treatment of the subject adumbrates some of the current "principles," e.g.:

[2] Robert K. Merton, *Social Theory and Social Structure* (Glencoe, Ill.: The Free Press of Glencoe, Illinois, 1949), p. 10.

He [the school superintendent] must constantly remember that he represents the whole community and not any part or fraction of it, and he must deal equal justice to all. As the representative of the whole community he will be wise not to ally himself at all closely with any faction, or division, or party in it.

He must, out of his larger knowledge, see clearly what are the attainable goals of the school system, and how best and how fast to attempt to reach them. From his larger knowledge, too, he must frequently reach up out of the routine of school supervision and executive duties into the higher levels of educational statesmanship. As a statesman, too, he must know how to take advantage of time and opportunity to carry his educational policy into effect.[3]

During the depression, when education along with other institutions was coming under close scrutiny, Jesse Newlon conceived of educational administration as social policy-making:

An adequate theory of school administration has never been developed in the United States. Down to the present, schools have largely been used as instruments for social control in terms of the maintenance of the status quo. Conditions of the twentieth century demand that they serve a creative as well as a conservative purpose.[4]

This creative purpose was that of directing the course of society, through educational institutions, toward the "democratic" ideal. This period also saw the "Dare the Schools Change the Social Order" theory of education rise to prominence. The school administrator was regarded primarily as both an educator and a political leader.

Twelve years later Mort, as he tried his hand at both academic study and the solution of practical problems in the field, complained that he found himself baffled by the lack of an encompassing theory:

[3] Ellwood P. Cubberley, *Public School Administration* (Boston: Houghton Mifflin Company, 1916), pp. 138–39.
[4] Jesse H. Newlon, *Educational Administration as Social Policy* (New York: Charles Scribner's Sons, 1934), pp. 76–77.

No such theory has been at hand either as a basis for appraisal of the solutions of others or as a tool for illuminating the novel problems I myself have faced. It has seemed to me that the literature of our field has been piecemeal. To no small degree it is made up of rules of thumb collected from hither and yon. . . . What I have felt the need of is a set of internally consistent principles covering the whole range of administration.[5]

Beginning with the assumption that educational administration is largely a very special form of local public administration with an extremely tenuous ministerial relationship to state departments of education, Mort developed a series of principles, which he classified under four categories: (1) those concerned with purpose; (2) those having their roots in common sense and prudence; (3) those derived from empirical knowledge; and (4) those arising out of balanced judgment. Under principles of purpose, he touches on the ancient problem of the relation of ends and means and apparently despairs of distinguishing between the two; school administrators apparently must be concerned with ends and means as an entity and be both yogis and commissars.[6] The purposes of education have little practical meaning apart from the devices that are employed to attain them,[7] and, presumably, the devices have little significance apart from purpose. The question arises at this point: Are the purpose of education and the purposes of administration identical? One fails to find a recognition of this distinction in Mort.

The common-sense principles, although not precisely formulated, deserve the serious consideration of all students of educational administration; for here Mort has recognized an aspect of administration which may come close, perhaps perilously close

[5] Paul R. Mort, *Principles of School Administration* (New York: McGraw-Hill Book Company, 1946), p. vii. See, also, the second edition, by Paul R. Mort and Donald H. Ross, 1947.

[6] See Arthur Koestler's, *The Yogi and the Commissar* (New York: The Macmillan Company, 1945).

[7] Mort, *Principles of School Administration*, pp. 15, 17.

for some who would eschew mere common sense, to providing a clue to its essential nature:

> It has been generally perceived that the understanding of the culture plays a very important part in determining the success of a school administrator. Sometimes it has even seemed to be the single determining factor. There are cases where school administrators have made a great success in spite of giving only a minimum of attention to the strictly educational phases of their job. Outstanding instances of this sort have given rise to much speculation on the value of professional training as we have known it for school administrators, particularly for larger cities. It has even led to the suggestion that the school superintendent should be comparatively a layman, on the assumption, presumably, that since a layman would not have the professional background he would necessarily have more space in his head for the general sense of the culture.[8]

These common-sense principles, which are classified under the headings "humanitarian," "prudential," and "tempo," are applied to the educational as well as to the administrative process. It is necessary, therefore, to assume that Mort does not believe that a theory of educational administration can be constructed about the administrative process per se. Nevertheless, it is possible to reformulate the common-sense principles in such a way that they apply only to the administrative process.

An entirely different approach to a theory of educational administration was made by Sears.[9] His inquiry into the administrative process was based on the assumption that administration is basically the same wherever it occurs, whether in educational or industrial organizations, in ecclesiastical or secular institutions, in public or private enterprises. Acknowledging his debt to the classic theorists in business and government administration—Henri Fayol, Frederick W. Taylor, and Luther H. Gulick—and finding no

[8] *Ibid.*, p. 93.
[9] Jesse B. Sears, *The Nature of the Administrative Process* (New York: McGraw-Hill Book Company, 1950).

reason to depart significantly from Fayol's original analysis of the administrative process,[10] Sears has identified the major functions of administration as planning, organizing, directing, co-ordinating, and controlling. After close scrutiny of the intricate relationships among these separate functions, he turned his attention to the power or authority that "energizes" the administrative act. He also makes important recommendations for further study: according to him the principal sources for the subject matter of educational administration are the social sciences, law, the science and art of administration, and the science of education; and the procedures should include viewing the administrative process as mechanism, process, and authority.[11]

Although intensely preoccupied with an analysis of administration, Sears was not entirely unmindful of the question of ends and purposes: "It seems evident that the problem of what to do must precede the problem of how to do it." [12] He was clearly aware, however, that the responsibility for formulating educational objectives does not belong exclusively to the subject matter of educational administration:

> It would be right to say that facts and principles pertaining to the problem of formulating educational objectives (for the nation, the state, the district, the school, the class, the child or professional organization) are administrative subject matter. But it is equally clear that political science, history of education, educational philosophy, and several other fields have an interest in these same problems, each from its special angle.[13]

[10] Henri Fayol, "The Administrative Theory in the State," in *Papers on the Science of Administration*, Luther H. Gulick and L. Urwick, eds. (New York: Institute of Public Administration, Columbia University, 1937), pp. 101–14. See also L. Urwick, "The Function of Administration: with Special Reference to the Work of Henri Fayol," in *Papers on the Science of Administration*, pp. 117–30.
[11] Sears, *The Nature of the Administrative Process*, pp. 488–92.
[12] *Ibid.*, p. 99.
[13] *Ibid.*, pp. 493–94.

Sears' analytical approach to the study of administration has been adopted by Hagman and Schwartz.[14] In their examination they renamed the elements as follows: leadership, purpose, organization, authority, group interaction, planning, communication, coordination, problem-solving, and evaluation. Somewhat less abstract than Sears, who held an *a priori* conception of the administrative process, Hagman and Schwartz are more specifically concerned with the duties of the educational administrator. They agree with Sears, however, in assuming that the administrative process is basically the same in all institutions; and they stress the need for theory:

> Fundamental to the maturing of public school administration as a field of professional activity in education is basic theory upon which the processes and procedure of administration can be built. Such basic theory is as yet undeveloped for the most part although signs of its emergence are sometimes to be observed. It is perhaps because of impatience with theorizing and because of eagerness to get at practical applications of our knowledge that we overlook the essential practicality of sound theory, out of which sound practice can be developed. Theory may, of course, have its genesis in practice as well as practice its genesis in theory.[15]

The most ambitious effort made so far to study educational administration is that of the Cooperative Program in Educational Administration.[16] For four years and at eight centers throughout the country, students attempted to study the phenomena of educational administration; and almost immediately they recognized the need for a general theory or theories. A continuing project is now under way with the avowed objective of formulating such a

---

[14] Harlan L. Hagman and Alfred Schwartz, *Administration in Profile for School Executives* (New York: Harper & Brothers, 1955).

[15] *Ibid.*, p. 296.

[16] For a brief, but good, description of this program, see John S. Carroll, "The Cooperative Program in Educational Administration and How It Grew," *Journal of Teacher Education*, III (June, 1952), 105–112.

The Theoretical Study of Educational Administration

theory.[17] Two aspects of the program are of interest to the student of administrative theory. First, an attempt is being made to clarify administrative functions and roles, e.g., a tentative list has been submitted as follows: the deliberative or policy-making role, the consultative or advising-on-the-basis-of-special-knowledge role, and the adjudicative or conflict-resolving role. Second, other disciplines such as law, sociology, and political science are being employed.

The trend toward theory in the practical field of administration is likely to continue. Coladarci and Getzels have insisted that theoretical considerations are necessary for successful practice and have proposed a theory of administration that views it as a "hierarchy of subordinate-superordinate relationships" (sic) within an institution or organization. In this relationship they have identified three dimensions: (1) the authority dimension, the source of which in education should be rational rather than traditional or charismatic; (2) the scope dimension, or the specific assignment of roles and functions; and (3) the affectivity dimension, or that of personal relationships.[18] This suggestion is strikingly reminiscent of Fayol, Gulick, and the classic theory of organization and administration. The "affectivity dimension" is new, but the recognition of hierarchy and functional specialization takes us back to the early theorists.

Preoccupied with urgent problems, the administrative craft has not been productive in the field of theory. A recognition of the need for theory has arisen, and from this recent interest many attempts to formulate systems of thought in this field may be expected. It is obvious that these rudimentary theorists, like Janus, are looking two ways: one school looks inward, analyzes the administrative process into its component parts, and attempts to establish a series of internal relations; and the second looks at administration from the point of view of its relations to the com-

[17] Francis S. Chase, "New Program in Administration," *The Elementary School Journal*, February, 1955, p. 311.
[18] Coladarci and Getzels, *The Use of Theory in Educational Administration*.

munity and to the intrinsic functions of the organization, so much so that one is compelled to ask whether or not administration is distinguishable from education. This initial divergence raises many questions. The most haunting one is: Can a comprehensive theory be constructed that will provide for a synthesis of the external and internal relations of administration? Also, one may well ask at the outset: What is the evidence for believing that administration can be considered *sui generis*, something that is separable from the other functions of an organization, and that possesses common elements regardless of the organization it serves? If the answer to this question is in the affirmative, it should be possible to construct a general theory that would lay bare the logical order of the administrative world. If, on the other hand, the nature and purposes of an organization so influence the character of administration that it is almost entirely different in business, for example, than it is in education, it will profit us little to concern ourselves with administration as such. This question lends itself to an empirical test.

Some insight, as well as consolation, may be derived from a brief inquiry into the field of public administration, where our consanguinity is attested to by their concern about the lack of theory, and about the difficulties involved in abstracting the administrative process from other aspects of government. There the lack of theory, and, earlier, the lack of normative principles, is regarded as a serious handicap for both practice and study. In 1887 Woodrow Wilson, whose religious and academic background allowed him small patience with the dross of politics in government administration, urged the adoption of the "lasting maxims of political wisdom" and "the permanent truths of political progress" in the field. He recommended the study of administration in order to "secure executive methods from the confusion and costliness of empirical experiment and set them upon foundations laid deep in stable principles." [19] Today, even those students of public admin-

[19] Woodrow Wilson, "The Study of Administration," *Political Science Quarterly*, II (June, 1887), 210.

istration who see their immediate task as one of accumulating reliable descriptive data, are looking forward to the possibility of being able to formulate comprehensive theories.[20]

About the second question—whether administration can be dealt with as a separate phenomenon—we find a greater concern among the political scientists than is exhibited by students of education. Gaus raised the question: ". . . is there a field of administration that can be abstracted from the services and the functions performed?" and he answered it in the negative: "A theory of public administration means in our time a theory of politics also."[21] Others have despaired of developing a scientific theory, even if administration is theoretically distinguishable from other functions of an organization. Dahl contended that the number and complexity of the variables to be controlled and the predominance of normative and value decisions in public administration practically make such a theory impossible.[22]

There are those who have advocated the study of administration as such, and, for the most part, they have foreseen the development of a science of administration. The work of Fayol has already been mentioned and it is familiar to all students in the field. In an address before the Second International Congress of Administrative Science at Brussels in 1923, he proposed the nearest thing we have to a comprehensive theory: the recognition of the importance of management in all organizations and the increase of that importance with the increase in size and complexity of the undertaking; an analysis of administrative operations; and the proposal of the structure necessary for administration to function effectively.[23]

---

[20] See William Anderson and John M. Gaus, *Research in Public Administration* (Chicago: Public Administration Service, 1945).

[21] John M. Gaus, "Trends in the Theory of Administration," *Public Administration Review*, x (Summer, 1950), 161–68.

[22] Robert A. Dahl, "The Science of Public Administration: Three Problems," *Public Administration Review*, vii (Winter, 1947), 1 ff.

[23] *Ibid.*; also Henri Fayol, "The Administrative Theory in the State," in *Papers on the Science of Administration*.

Willoughby went so far as to assume that there are fundamental scientific principles of administration analogous to those in the physical sciences and that public administration can become a science.[24] A great deal of the current opinion on the subject follows in this vein; the first step in the development of administrative theory is the formulation of hypotheses stated in precise causal relationships, the testing of which will yield a body of empirical data from which it will be possible to extend theoretical formations.[25]

In addition to these comparatively conservative approaches to the development of administrative theory there has been abroad for some years a much more spectacular theory about the function, importance, and power of administration. Taking its departure from Fayol's thesis that the increasing number, size, and complexity of the organizations in modern society demand more, and more efficient, administration, this theory assumes that the administrative function will be preëminent in a highly organized society. Adams, who saw the necessity for an administrative elite to replace the capitalistic one, defined the essential nature of administration:

> Administration is the capacity of coordinating many, and often conflicting, social energies in a single organism, so adroitly that they shall act as a unity. This presupposes the power of recognizing a series of relations between numerous special social interests, with all of which no single man can be intimately acquainted. Probably no very highly specialized class can be strong in this intellectual quality because of the intellectual isolation incident to specialization; and yet administration or

[24] W. F. Willoughby, "The Science of Administration," in *Essays in Political Science*, J. M. Matthews and John Hart, eds. (Baltimore: The Johns Hopkins University Press, 1937).

[25] See Edwin O. Stene, "An Approach to a Science of Administration," *The American Political Science Review*, xxxiv (December, 1940), 1124–37; Luther H. Gulick, "Science, Values, and Public Administration," in *Papers on the Science of Administration*, pp. 191–95; and Simon, *Administrative Behavior*, pp. 20–44.

The Theoretical Study of Educational Administration

generalization is not only the faculty upon which social stability rests, but is, possibly, the highest faculty of the human mind.[26]

The influence of Adams is apparent in Burnham, who predicted the inevitable rise of a managerial elite. The managers were to become the new aristocracy, excelling in prestige and power the statesmen, the capitalists, the scholars, and all other classes and professions. In his view the nature of modern technological society makes managers indispensable, and, as society becomes more dependent on them, they will gradually gain control of policy-making powers.[27]

In this brief review of the literature on administrative theory we have found no well-formulated theories with their attendant orthodox believers, schismatics, and heretics. But there are the dim outlines of three theories that may be emerging. The first of these arises from the assumption that the administrative function cannot be abstracted from the other functions of the educational organization. From this assumption it follows that the educational administrator must be a teacher, a scholar, or an educator. While he has administrative duties and responsibilities, these are so closely related to the purposes and processes of education that they cannot be understood or performed adequately apart from the intrinsic educational activities of the organization. As an educator, the educational administrator is not and cannot be restricted to purely administrative tasks, but he engages in the same professional activities as the teacher, the counselor, the scholar, and the researcher. He is primarily a specialist in education, or in some academic discipline, rather than in administration per se; and he is on part, or full-time, assignment to attend to the administrative aspects of his profession, which involve primary considerations of education. Thus, a philosopher of education such as

[26] Brooks Adams, *The Theory of Social Revolutions* (New York: The Macmillan Company, 1913).

[27] James Burnham, *The Managerial Revolution* (New York: The John Day Company, 1941).

William Torrey Harris might become a superintendent of schools with the strong conviction that his principal responsibilities lie in the fields of the improvement of instructional techniques, curriculum reform, research, and philosophy, and only secondarily in the area of management. If the administrative or management duties become too onerous, such an administrator would distribute them among other teachers. Since educational administration can never be divorced from education, even for the purpose of study, it is not likely that this theory would ever consider as possible a science of educational administration, *qua* administration. Administrative personnel in education are to be regarded as teachers, not a separate administrative class; although presumably they might emerge as educational statesmen or politicians.

The second theory which may be emerging centers around the regard for administration as a function that can be abstracted from the other functions of an organization and the belief that its nature is essentially the same in all organizations. Following the lead of Fayol, Gulick, Sears, and Stene, this general view is hopeful that the elements of administration may be unambiguously identified, and that it will be possible to formulate the test hypotheses about causal relations. For example, the psychological principles that apply to working with people in groups in industry would be applicable to working with people in educational organizations, or the line-and-staff organization might prove to be the most effective way of administering all organizations. This type of theory would provide ultimately, if not now, for an administrative class, specialists in administration rather than in education, who conceivably would be interchangeable from one type of institution to another. The relation of this type of administrator and his purely administrative functions to the other functions of an organization is nowise clearly anticipated, although much of the argument about the relation of policy-making and the execution of policy undoubtedly foreshadows the intricate and difficult adjustments that would be necessary.

A third emergent theory is one that is, perhaps, often unwittingly adopted. If it were explicitly stated it would read something like this: Education, along with other institutions in society, has become tremendously complex, heterogeneous, unwieldy, and competitive. This state of affairs has given rise to the need for administrators who can see the various components in relation to one another and, also, can insure the survival of educational organizations. So important is this function for the prevention of chaos and disintegration that the person who knows how to run an educational enterprise should also have, and, as a matter of fact, will have, a great deal to say about the purposes for which it is run. The specialist may provide the administrator with facts and technical information, but decisions about the purposes of education and the methods required to accomplish these purposes should be left to the administrator, whose mind can encompass the complex and far-reaching effects of such decisions. Practical decisions under such a theory would probably be guided by the demands of organization and the conditions of its survival and growth. The intrinsic functions of the organization are in such deep insolvency to administration that they must be deferential. This is the theory of the managerial revolution applied to education.

These three dim and emergent theories having been clarified, one of them—the second of those mentioned above—shall be carried forward. At this point the major propositions that will be developed in subsequent chapters are presented in outline form.

I. Administration is a phenomenon that can be unambiguously identified and defined; it can be distinguished from the other functions of an organization; it is basically the same in all organizations, whether they be educational, industrial, governmental, military, or ecclesiastical.

II. The essential nature of the administrative process has been identified by Fayol, Gulick, Sears, and others who belong to the school of thought that administration is an activity that can be studied in its own right. However, they have neglected to give adequate consideration to the human and personal relationships involved and have not attempted to include in their theories the relations of the administrative function to the intrinsic activity of the organization, on the one hand, and to the community at large, on the other.

III. Administration came into being with the first organized activity; its growth can be explained largely by the increased size, number, and complexity of organizations, and by the increase in the variety, speed, and urgency of the activities within the organization. Increased administration, due to organizational demands, in turn contributes to the complexity of the organization and demands even more administration. If, as has been suggested, administration is increased for its own sake, which is possible, it can create a complexity that appears to demand even additional administrative activity.

IV. The administrative function requires a specific structure within an organization in order to operate effectively, and it demands specific abilities on the part of the administrator.

V. The larger social role of administration consists in providing stability for organizations and, indirectly, for society at large. This responsibility is accomplished through the elucidation and clarification of organizational purposes and objectives and through the maintenance of organizations in order to avoid both the waste of social energies necessary for their formation and the imbalance that will occur when organizations fail to accomplish their objectives. Concomitant effects of the extensive operation of administration may be expected.

VI. The nature of the administrative process, which is demanded by organization, is antithetical to the intrinsic functions of some organizations. In educational institutions this incompatibility is greater than it is in industry and less than it is in research institutions and in schools devoted exclusively to the creative arts, for example. However, since all organizations depend upon administration for their survival and maintenance, the solution to the problem inevitably involves some compromise between administrative necessity and educational activity.

CHAPTER III

the Administrative process

THE FIRST TASK in the development of our comprehensive theory of educational administration is that of definition. To some this is an arid region to be traversed as quickly as possible before the specter of the nominalist-realist controversy is revived. However, since definition is an intellectual activity of high order and absolutely essential to our purposes, we should not permit the scandal of its ancient excesses to stain its present reputation. We may assume that our definition of administration affirms some kind of reality, but more important for our immediate purposes, we intend that it will serve as an unambiguous subject for discourse and investigation.

The Problem of Definition

Administration has been recognized as a phenomenon that attaches itself to all organizations and institutions—government, business, armies, schools, churches, art museums, hospitals, libraries, and research foundations—in which people work together for the attainment of organizational objectives and, what is frequently overlooked, for the realization of certain individual objectives, which can be achieved only through some form of organizational identification. An initial and debatable assumption is made here that this phenomenon can be singled out and defined as an item of knowable reality; that is possesses the requisite distinctive characteristics to be recognizable in any type of organization; and that it is more than a mere construct in that its relations with other phenomena may be systematically observed. Educational administration, therefore, is assumed to be the same activity as administration in other types of organizations; and a definition of educational administration is a definition of administration in general. This is our first major theoretical assumption.[1]

The problem of definition is complicated in this instance by the fact that administration has been defined, but, as is so often true in the study of social phenomena, the definition is both vague and ambiguous. "Administration" does have a dictionary meaning. This indicates that it is used with some degree of precision and satisfaction. The student, therefore, is hardly free to indulge in an irresponsible or idiosyncratic use of the term. But, although the philosophical tension about the making of definitions may have relaxed in recent years, the responsibility for reducing vagueness and ambiguity continues. This responsibility cannot be discharged entirely by coining new terms or by offering purely stipulative definitions for old terms—practices that seem to have considerable vogue in some quarters, where there is great audacity in inventing new words and new meanings for familiar words—but rather by making current lexical definitions more precise than they are. This responsibility was recognized by Irving Babbitt in his strictures against "romanticism":

[1] For a similar opinion from educators, see Will French, J. Dan Hull, and B. L. Dodds, *American High School Administration* (New York: Rinehart & Company, 1951), p. 4.

But this inability or unwillingness to define may in itself turn out to be only one aspect of a movement that from Rousseau to Bergson has sought to discredit the analytical intellect—what Wordsworth calls 'the false secondary power by which we multiply distinctions.' However, those who are with Socrates rather than with Rousseau or Wordsworth in this matter, will insist on the importance of definition, especially in a chaotic era like the present; for nothing is more characteristic of such an era than its irresponsible use of general terms. Now to measure up to the Socratic standard, a definition must not be abstract and metaphysical, but experimental; it must not, that is, reflect our opinion of what a word should mean, but what it actually has meant. Mathematicians may be free at times to frame their own definitions, but in the case of words like classic and romantic, that have been used innumerable times, and used not in one but in many countries, such a method is inadmissible. One must keep one's eye on actual usage. One should indeed allow for a certain amount of freakishness in this usage. Beaumarchais, for example, makes classic synonymous with barbaric (*Essai sur le genre chamatique séneux*). One may disregard an occasional alienation of this kind, but if one can find only confusion and inconsistency in all the main uses of words like classic and romantic, the only procedure for those who speak or write in order to be understood is to banish the words from their vocabulary.[2]

Social scientists, like mathematicians, should be free to frame new definitions for new concepts; but in the case of a word like "administration," which has acquired meanings, the lexical definition cannot be ignored. This is what Fowler meant by "usage": "The word "usage" conveyed the combined obligations—the social one of pleasing by simplicity and clarity and suitability of language; and the intellectual one of respect for tradition and reason through a conscious choice of the best forms." [3]

The problem here, then, is that of more precise definition. This

---

[2] Irving Babbit, *Rousseau and Romanticism* (New York: Meridian Books, 1955 [first published in 1919]), pp. 16–17.

[3] Jacques Barzun, "Fowler's Generation," *The American Scholar*, xxvi, No. 3 (Summer, 1957), 316.

task can be performed, first, by discovering the basic unambiguous elements in the lexical definitions and those in common use, or what one may call the area of maximum agreement as to usage; and, second, by determining which borderland conditions are implied in this definition and which are not. To be sure, there is a stipulative procedure involved; but the core of the lexical definition provides the logical basis for the extension of its boundaries. Whatever arbitrariness is involved is dictated by the definition in common usage. This procedure will become clear as an attempt is made to define administration.

A review of the definitions of administration reveals that they contain a common set of functions or conditions. Administration is: (1) the carrying out of policies that have been determined and accepted; (2) the direction of the efforts of people working together in their reciprocal relations so that the ends of the organization may be accomplished; and (3) the maintenance of organization. Fayol's analysis of the administrative process into the five functions of planning, organizing, commanding, co-ordinating, and controlling,[4] and Gulick's restatement of these functions as planning, organizing, staffing, directing, co-ordinating, reporting, and budgeting, are attempts to break the administrative activity down into its component parts.[5] Students who have criticized this definition and these analyses have done so because they failed to see how the administrative process could be separated from the other activities of the organization, or because they thought that the human and psychological factors had been omitted.[6] But it is almost universally accepted that, whatever else the administrative activity may do, it does include the functions identified in the above definitions.

[4] Henri Fayol, "The Administrative Theory in the State," in *Papers on the Science of Administration*, Luther H. Gulick and L. Urwick, eds. (New York: Institute of Public Administration, Columbia University, 1937), pp. 101–14.

[5] Luther H. Gulick, "Notes on the Theory of Organization," in *Papers on the Science of Administration*, pp. 3–45.

[6] See Herbert A. Simon, *Administrative Behavior* (New York: The Macmillan Company, 1955), pp. 35–36.

The Administrative Process

To be sure, the sphere of the administrative activity has been extended by definition from time to time to include other functions. Is the formulation or modification of an organization's purposes a part of the administrative function? When does public relations cease to be administration and become politics? These functions under certain conditions are called administrative, but the conditions have not been clearly described. An attempt shall be made to reduce the ambiguity in these borderland areas.

Let us accept the consensus of definitions that, whatever else administration may be, it is at least the activity that concerns itself with the survival and maintenance of an organization and with the direction of the activities of people working within the organization in their reciprocal relations to the end that the organization's purposes may be attained. This somewhat oversimplified definition, then, provides the basis for selecting the functions that may be called administrative; and in it there are several obvious implications for our inquiry. Prerequisite or at least concomitant to administration is organization. Administration is directly responsible, not for performing the work of an organization, but for attending to its performance; administration in business and industry neither produces nor sells goods, nor does educational administration teach geography. Since administration is charged with the responsibility for the attainment of organizational objectives, it follows that the administrator should know what the objectives are. The assumptions are implicit in the lexical definition of administration; they may be instrumental in making the definition even more precise.

It follows from the definition given above that any activity that is performed to maintain an organization or to direct the activities of people working within an organization toward the accomplishments of the organization's objectives may be classified as administrative in nature. Planning, fund-raising, public relations, and leadership may logically be classified as administration when, and only when, they occur under the above conditions. If, for example, a superintendent of schools engages in lobbying for funds to support a program of education that has been legislated, or clearly decided upon by a policy-making body, he is performing an administrative act; but if he attempts to persuade a state legislature to enact laws changing the accepted purposes of the schools, he is not engaging in administration. If any one of the above-named activities is employed to modify the purposes of an organization, it cannot, according to our definition, be regarded as administrative in nature, nor would we expect persons who are referred to as administrators to be successfully engaged in them.

If we pursue this conclusion, we shall encounter such questions as: When the purposes of an organization are changed in order that the organization survive and prosper, is this activity administration? Since this situation is probably not uncommon,[7] we should decide whether it logically belongs to our definition of administration. If we say that administration is the activity that serves to sustain an organization and to direct its internal energies in such a way that the purposes of the organization may be attained, then it is indisputable that changing the purposes of an organization, even in order to prolong organizational life, is not a part of administration. It is conceivable that an organization might exist for the purpose of modifying another organization's objectives, or that changes in purpose are an organization's objectives, as they may well be in education. Then it becomes an administrative responsibility to provide the mechanisms whereby such changes may be effected.

Within our definition there are really two types of activities: (1) those concerned with the direction of the activities of persons working within an organization, which are labeled co-ordinating activities, and which can hardly be described under any circumstances as other than administrative; and (2) activities such as public relations, which are administrative in nature when they are employed for the accomplishment of accepted purposes. This definition reduces immediately the ambiguity in the use of the concept of administration and should permit more clearly for-

[7] See Burton R. Clark's "Organizational Adaptation and Precarious Values: A Case Study," *American Sociological Review*, XXI, No. 3 (June, 1956), 327–36.

mulated hypotheses of relationships. Also, we are assuming that it corresponds in large measure to the activity pursued by persons called administrators.

So wide an acceptance has our definition of administration gained in the common interpretation that when a person occupying a position that is regarded as administrative becomes known for activities other than the ones we have specified, he is remembered primarily not as an administrator but for the other things he did. Horace Mann, for example, is remembered as an educator, a philosopher, or a statesman in the field of education, but rarely does one read or hear of him as an "administrator." Here the common usage of the wayfaring man is more realistic perhaps than some of the theories of the learned. The fact that famous statesmen, philosophers, and scholars have occupied administrative positions has given rise to the idea that haunts the minds of educational administrators today—that they should all be educational statesmen.

In other fields, also, the common usage respects the distinction between the administrative activity and other functions which are sometimes performed by the same person. In ecclesiastical administration a bishop or a moderator may be regarded as a brilliant theologian, an eloquent preacher, and a poor administrator, excellent in all three, or merely a good administrator. An industrialist who decides the purposes of an organization and then attends to their attainment is regarded both as an entrepreneur and as an administrator. A public official holding an administrative position who engages predominantly in pursuits other than those required to carry out legislative policy soon comes to be regarded as a politician. The fact that administrators who have been theologians, scholars, statesmen, or entrepreneurs are remembered as one of the latter may be due to the fact that in the past the administrative function was not so important to society as it is today. Or it may be due to the fact that the records of administrative achievements are more perishable, less tangible, or simply less spectacular.

If by this time the reader has become somewhat fearful that our definition of administration will leave it a rather modest, paltry thing, this fear should vanish when the range and importance of the administrative task are described in greater detail. For example, our theory holds that it is not an administrative responsibility to modify the purposes of the educational organization, and this would appear, at first glance, to be a diminution of the administrative function. However, our theory does hold that it is an administrative responsibility to apprehend purposes and to discern any changes that are taking place in them. This function alone calls for great social skill and perception, and it is tremendously important in our society. We shall return in subsequent chapters to the methods and techniques of apprehending the public will for education and to the role of administration in modern society. Having undoubtedly raised the controversial question about the separation of administration from over-all policy-making, we shall at this point attempt to clarify our distinction on theoretical grounds.

Administrative and Purpose Decisions Theoretically Distinguished

It has been a principle of some repute in the study of education that a clear separation between policy formation and administrative action is essential to effective organization; [8] and earlier students of public administration also recognized the same principle.[9] The phrase "policy formation" we shall interpret to mean the setting

[8] See, for example, Alonzo G. Grace, "The State and the Educational System," in *Changing Conceptions in Educational Administration*, The Forty-Fifth Yearbook, Part II (Chicago: The National Society for the Study of Education, 1946), p. 15.

[9] See, for example, Frank J. Goodnow, *Politics and Administration* (New York: The Macmillan Company, 1900), p. 22.

up of the purposes of an organization, making choices between conflicting purposes, and modifying established purposes. Given such a definition, we accept the distinction that has traditionally been made between policy-making and the execution of policy, a distinction that is now regarded in some circles as arbitrary and unrealistic. Furthermore, we shall attempt to show that such a distinction is theoretically sound.

First of all, we must reckon with the so-called apostles of realism, particularly in the field of public administration, who assert that actually it is impossible to distinguish clearly between policy-making decisions and decisions effecting them and that the execution of policy is the essence of it.[10] Their assertions, in some instances, are much less dogmatic than they appear at first glance, and, apparently, they are based on no sounder theoretical evidence than the separation-of-functions theory that we propose. One student admits that it has long been customary to distinguish between policy-making and policy execution, but he insists that the distinction has value only as a matter of relative emphasis:

> Public policy, to put it flatly, is a continuous process, the formation of which is inseparable from its execution. Public policy is being formed as it is being executed, and it is being executed as it is being formed. Politics and administration play a continuous role in both formation and execution, though there is probably more politics in the formation of policy, more administration in the execution of it.
>
> It is characteristic of our age that most legislation is looked upon as policy deciding. Hence policy making in the broad sense is not supposed to be a part of administration. While these propositions are true in a general way, they tend to obscure two important facts, namely, 1, that many policies are not ordained with a stroke of a legislative or dictatorial pen but

[10] See, for example, Simon, *Administrative Behavior*, pp. 52–61; Dwight Waldo, *The Administrative State* (New York: The Ronald Press Company, 1948), Chap. 7; and Carl Joachim Friedrich, "Public Policy and the Nature of Administrative Responsibility," in *Public Policy*, Carl Joachim Friedrich and Edward S. Mason, eds. (Cambridge, Mass.: Harvard University Press, 1940).

evolve slowly over long periods of time, and, 2, that administrative officials participate continuously and significantly in this process of evolving policy.[11]

Although he denies that an absolute separation between policy-making and policy execution is possible, the author of the above quotation admits that there is likely to be more administration in the execution of policy than in its formation. The tendency toward the separation is admitted.

The despair among students of public administration that attends the running of the line of demarcation between policy and administrative decisions is indicated by the following quotation from Woodrow Wilson:

> No lines of demarcation, setting apart administrative from non-administrative functions, can be run between this and that department of government without being run up hill and down dale, over dizzy heights of distinction and through dense jungles of statutory enactment, hither and thither, around "ifs" and "buts," "whens" and "howevers," until they become altogether lost to the common eye not accustomed to this sort of surveying, and consequently not acquainted with the use of the theodolite of logical discernment.[12]

If it is true that the theoretical distinction between over-all policy-making and the execution of such policy is functionally meaningless, we shall be forced to abandon our separation-of-powers theory; but before we capitulate to this view, we shall endeavor to see if we can establish some kind of theoretical justification for a view that has the *consensus gentium* in its favor and we shall expect that from such a theory hypotheses may be drawn that can be tested empirically.

Two complicating practical aspects need to be clarified. First, there is the fact that both over-all policy-making and the administrative function as we have defined it have been performed

---

[11] Friedrich, "Public Policy and The Nature of Administrative Responsibility," in *Public Policy*, pp. 6–7.
[12] Woodrow Wilson, "The Study of Administration," *Political Science Quarterly*, II (June, 1887), 213.

The Administrative Process

often by the same person. Educational organizations, like many other types of organizations, have, at times, been private enterprises and, as such, have been owned and operated by the same person. In these instances it has not been necessary to attempt the separation of the two functions because there has been no question of jurisdiction. One person possesses the responsibility for, and is capable of, performing both functions. It certainly does not follow that the two functions are inseparable. Because a person performing both functions may normally be referred to as an administrator today may be a tribute to the rising status of the administrative function, but it does not exclude the possibility that he is acting as an entrepreneur also.

Another aspect of educational administration that does not directly affect our theory of the separation of over-all policy-making from its execution, but that may impinge on it and certainly complicates the task of identifying the administrative function, is the nature of the intrinsic functions of the educational organization. The relationship between these functions—teaching, counseling, and related activities—is a complicated one and will be given extended consideration later on. It will suffice here to point out that teaching and administration have often been done by the same person, and, therefore, whatever influence the teaching function has had on over-all policy-making has become associated with administration also. Since few school superintendents and college presidents do any teaching today, the distinction between teaching and administration is becoming more pronounced in spite of the feverish efforts to prevent their sunderance.

To help establish the theoretical distinction between the administrative process and over-all policy or purpose formation, we shall first look at administration in its most primitive form. The often-quoted example of two men rolling a stone [13] illustrates

[13] Herbert A. Simon, Donald W. Smithburg, and Victor A. Thompson, *Public Administration* (New York: Alfred A. Knopf, 1950), p. 3. "When two men cooperate to roll a stone that neither could have moved alone, the rudiments of administration have appeared."

the simplest kind of administration. Two men decide to combine their efforts to roll a stone. The decision to move the stone has been made by them or by someone else, but in either case this decision is not administrative in nature so far as the stone-rolling organization is concerned. Both men then co-operate to roll the stone away from its location and, perhaps, to a designated spot; and one of them, at the same time that he is engaged in rolling the stone, attempts to direct the efforts of the other person in relation to his own. In the latter capacity he is performing administration, although he continues to perform the intrinsic work of the simple organization that has developed.

In the example given above the organization is simple and somewhat absurd. In order to avoid giving the impression of great naivete, we should indicate briefly at this point the complicated nature of the relationship between administration and organization. The question will inevitably arise, what happens to this theoretical separation of powers if the stone-moving operation, including the decisions to move the stone and to choose its new location, is a means to some more inclusive end such as clearing land for building or cultivation? In this event all the decisions are administrative in nature, i.e., they are concerned with means rather than with ends or purposes. How then may one distinguish between them? If administration is a knowable reality, what are the identifying criteria in the above illustration? In one instance we have stated that the decision to move the stone is a purpose decision and in another the same decision appears to be administrative, although we should note that the direction of the efforts of the persons moving the stone is regarded as an administrative act in both situations. The answers to these questions become obvious if we realize that administration is not found apart from organizations. Therefore, we must identify the organization—the host of administration—in order to apply our criteria of identification of the administrative act. If we have an organization, i.e., a system of directed activities of two or more persons whose purpose it is to move stones, then both the stone-movers and the

The Administrative Process

director must accept in some degree the purpose of the organization. The fact that this organization may be a relatively permanent one or extremely ephemeral does not alter its essential nature. Nor is its nature affected by the fact that it may be a component of a larger, more or less formal organization, since all organizations, except perhaps society itself, inevitably are.

It does not require a great deal of imagination to see how this organizational analysis may be applied to a complex educational system. The purposes of such a system are determined largely by individuals and groups outside the organization proper. It is true that teachers, specialists of various types, and administrators within the system may contribute to such purpose-making, but they do so as citizens or as contributors of specialized information. The means to accomplish these purposes are then adopted by the administration of the inclusive educational organization. These means then may become purposes for some of the smaller units within the system. For example, the administration of a school system may decide that homogeneous grouping should be adopted as a means to secure certain accepted purposes. Such a decision is purely administrative. This means may then become a purpose for the testing division, and its director may in turn devise means to accomplish it. He is likely to have contributed information to the higher echelons of administration about some of the problems involved in homogeneous grouping, but he is usually not the one to make the decision to adopt it. Distinctions such as this are easily made, comprehensible, and logical, even in such close-fitting and overlapping series of organizations as we have described. This fact adds cogency to our argument that the administrative process may be identified independently of the purpose or over-all policy-making function. Closer philosophical scrutiny of administrative decisions will make our theory abundantly clear.

Simon [14] has introduced the interesting suggestion that the study of the relation between over-all policy-making and the execution of policy may be approached through a value-fact schema that

[14] See his *Administrative Behavior*, particularly Chaps. III and IV.

apparently has some correspondence—but not equivalence—to the ends-mean continuum. However, apparently he does not believe that the separation can be rigidly maintained in administrative decisions. We are aware that Simon is still on the side of the preponderance of modern opinion, but we are bold to suggest that if we analyze administrative decisions we should find them comparatively devoid of value choices, and, therefore, if this is true, we should assume that they have little to do with changing the purposes of an organization. In the last section of this chapter, we shall present some evidence about and impressions of the administrative role that tend to substantiate this view, but here we wish to clarify the relation of value choices to organizational purposes.

Administrators have usually accepted sometime prior to their becoming administrators the purposes and over-all policies of the school organizations that they serve. This acceptance may be conscious or unconscious, but an administrator usually becomes an "organization man" *à outrance*. This original commitment to organizational purposes affects the nature of administrative decisions. Since purpose is a possibility suffused with continuing value, any decision affecting purpose must involve *de novo* value choices. But since original value choices may continue and do not have to be made anew each time a decision about facts is made, the ends-means continuum may operate at all times without requiring that a decision be made about ends each time one is made about means. An administrative decision contains a purpose element, compounded of value and possibility, that is not of the nature of a choice—although it may contain genuine value choices that do not affect the perseverating purpose commitment—and it always includes a decisive element about matters of fact. Such decisions usually contain two antecedents, implicit value commitments, and a nonvaluational comparative factual decision.

Let us analyze an administrative decision in education to illustrate what we mean: A school superintendent decides that the whole word method of teaching reading will be used in a school system rather than the phonics method because it is "better." This decision is a purely factual one and involves no relevant value choices. The word "better" in this case is deceptive. The superintendent has long since accepted the purposes of the school, one of which is the teaching of Johnny to read. That it is "good" for Johnny to learn to read is a value that does not require a decision here. It is an antecedent value commitment. The second such commitment is that this end should be accomplished with as little cost or as efficiently as possible. Hence the term "better" is applied to the whole word method. The only real choice in this decision is one based upon facts or alleged facts. Numerous value choices, irrelevant to the attainment of the objectives, may, of course, be made.

The example given above is simple enough. Let us now extend this analysis to a decision involving an apparent conflict in values and purposes. If teaching Johnny to read by an otherwise efficient method proves, or even threatens, to be injurious to his health, it obviously will not be adopted. Again there is no value choice in this decision because it has long since been made. The superintendent not only holds the purposes of the organization in mind when he makes his decisions, but he also has them arranged in a hierarchy. The purposes of the schools include both literacy and health for Johnny and the saving of resources; and they are arranged in a hierarchy of organizational purposes that the school administrator accepts and in light of which he makes his decisions.

We cannot say that the administrator is never faced with decisions about the acceptance, change, or abolition of purposes in the educational organization. Purposes jostle one another for higher positions in the hierarchy: What comparative status will teaching for academic knowledge, training for vocational skills, and educating for social adjustment have among the school's responsibilities? Such questions, we believe, are decided not by administrators, although they may contribute to the decisions, but by educators from all ranks—teachers, counselors, supervisors, research workers, and professors—and by business men, parents, politicians, welfare workers, philosophers, and knights errant in education either as organized policy-making bodies or as individuals or groups influencing the administrator. As the purposes of the organization change, the administrator does make value choices, and it is our theory that he either accepts the modifications in purposes or moves to another organization.

If our theory that administrative decisions typically are decisions of fact made in the light of existing values and purposes is correct, we should be able to prove it by an analysis of administrative decisions. Cursory observation makes our theory plausible: educational administrators are usually regarded as conformists and chary about taking a stand on controversial issues;[15] and a few straightforward accounts of their actual duties reveal how exclusively their decisions are concerned with means.[16] A more systematic study would probably reveal that administrative decisions are largely factual and that the difficulty is due to both the obscure nature of the facts with which they deal, e.g., what is the most efficient method of teaching Johnny to read, and the difficulty in apprehending the hierarchical order of purposes that the community holds for education.

The Warranting of Administrative Decisions

Administrative decisions contain three elements. First, there is a continuing element of purpose that gives direction to the decisions about means. Second, there is the actual decision about the choice of means to accomplish the accepted purposes. And third, there is usually a concomitant value choice in the selection of means that does not materially affect the end. We shall indicate briefly how each of these three elements may be validated.

[15] *The School Administrator*, April–May, 1956, p. 7.
[16] See, for example, Mark Scully, "A Day in the Life of One Superintendent," *Peabody Journal of Education*, xxxiv (March, 1956), 291–95, and C. S. Blackburn's "A Superintendent's Day," *Ibid.*, pp. 296–97.

The Administrative Process

The purpose element in administrative decisions may be warranted officially or personally. If, as we have assumed, most, if not all, administrators have accepted the objectives of the organizations in which they work, then in making their official decisions, they have simply to recall their original acceptances and to identify the changes in them that they have subsequently made as the objectives of the organizations changed. The only test here is how accurately they recall the original or identify the new objectives or purposes; and it is always and exclusively a test of fact. But in accepting the organizations' purposes in the first place and in acceding to changes in these original purposes, administrators have had to make personal value choices. It is the validation of these choices that we shall now discuss.

If a school administrator attempts to justify his choice to accept the educational objective of teaching people to be literate, he may assume uncritically that this decision is right for him because literacy brings certain individual and social consequences. He may, therefore, think that his original judgment is validated if he determines that these consequences ensue upon literacy. But the mere occurrence of these consequences does not determine whether they are good or bad, right or wrong, desirable, or undesirable. If he, in turn, attempts to justify the value of these consequences by more remote ones, the same fallacy occurs. Dahl has pointed out that all judgments about what should be done, after any number of factual justifications, are ultimately pushed back to an irreducible value consideration.[17] He failed to note explicitly, however, that nowhere along the continuum can a value judgment be warranted entirely by facts but only by the value of the facts. A normative criterion must be applied at every step, although it is a continuing one.

How, then, may the administrator warrant decisions of this kind? The criteria are varied and the same as those involved for all value judgments. Not only is it necessary for him to justify

[17] Robert A. Dahl, "The Science of Public Administration: Three Problems," *Public Administration Review*, vii (Winter, 1947), 1–2.

his decisions, but also he must select the method for their validation. He may invoke the moral law, or some other absolute of which he is as sure as he is of the starry heavens above, as the ultimate ground of valuation. He may use the hedonistic principle of the greatest happiness for the greatest number. He may decide that what is desired, or what is considered desirable generally, is, for him, desirable. Or he may count the cost and judge the value of the consequences in economic terms. If he attempts to judge his decision by the pragmatic consequences, he may suspect that he is substituting fact for value, unless he admits that certain values attach to consequences, and that it is his acceptances of these values that makes the consequences good. There is no universal agreement about the ultimate basis of the good—Schopenhauer would question the value of survival itself—and decisions about purposes can be warranted only by some kind of a personal acceptance of their value.[18]

Administrative decisions about means are warranted by facts or alleged facts. For example, method A of teaching history tends to increase the interest of students in contemporary problems, without sacrificing the learning of the basic facts of history; increased interest in contemporary problems is an accepted goal of the educational organization; therefore the adoption of method A is correct. Or, we may take another example: the probabilities are great that teachers with four years of college education will use more correct English in speaking to their classes than teachers with two years of college education; the community prefers teachers who use excellent grammar and diction, even if they

[18] For a variety of the modern methods of validating judgments of this kind, see G. E. Moore, *Principia Ethica* (Cambridge, England: Cambridge University Press, 1951); R. B. Perry, *Realms of Value* (Cambridge, Mass.: Harvard University Press, 1954); Abraham Edel, *Ethical Judgment* (Glencoe, Ill.: The Free Press of Glencoe, Illinois, 1955); W. D. Lamont, *The Value Judgment* (Edinburgh: University Press, 1955); Jacques Rueff, *From the Physical to the Social Sciences* (Baltimore: The Johns Hopkins University Press, 1929), Chap. xiv; and C. I. Lewis, *The Ground and Nature of the Right* (New York: Columbia University Press, 1951).

The Administrative Process

cost more; therefore the selection of teachers with four years of college is a correct administrative decision. The warranting of this aspect of an administrative decision can be done by determining the factual truth of the first two statements in each seriatim. An extended catalogue of more complicated examples would serve merely to illustrate that it is difficult to determine the facts.

In connection with the decisions about means, there are many opportunities for value choices that do not affect the objectives of the organization. If two procedures are equally effective insofar as the purposes of an organization are concerned, the administrator is free to choose the one for which he has an aesthetic or moral preference; and insofar as these decisions do not involve the purposes of the organization, or those of any other organization, they are warranted only by the taste and conscience of the individual administrator. He may prefer a green fountain pen to a black one for signing contracts. His decision in this case is validated only by his own preference.

While theoretically the warranting of decisions about means is easier than the warranting of purpose decisions, we would be unrealistic if we did not recognize the serious difficulties encountered in determining facts. To say that the administrator must often act on the basis of incomplete facts is an understatement. Most decisions are made on the basis of scant, obscure, and conflicting evidence; and some of the facts may be so illusive that they will never be known. But the administrator cannot wait until all the evidence is in. School must keep. He, therefore, makes his decisions largely on the basis of alleged fact.

The question arises at this point: What is the difference between a decision made on the basis of uncertain results and uncertainty even about the criteria for determining facts, and a decision in the realm of value where the methods of validation are varied and personal? There is both a logical and a practical distinction. The very decisions we make in the first instance contain the grounds for their own validation. For example, if the school superintendent makes a decision to have reading taught by the whole word method because such a method results in greater speed and comprehension, he has set the terms of judging the correctness of his decision. If, on the other hand, he justifies his decision on the basis of what is better for the student, he has not included the terms of validation. If, as is so often the case, he means by "better" another set of results, he may revert to another test of fact; but he is continuing to avoid setting the terms for a decision on his value judgment.

The second difference is practical. Today there is rather common consent that factual results are theoretically verifiable publicly and may be determined by measurement, observation of behavior, personal statements, and other accepted methods of recognition. There are people who refuse to accept facts that are obvious to most of us, but the "spectre of the stubborn man" is much less haunting under the light of verifiable empirical evidence than it is in the more shadowy realms of value, although the illumination of the former may be entirely artificial.

Conclusion

Administration has been defined as that activity which maintains an organization and directs its activities in their reciprocal relations toward the accomplishment of the organization's purposes. Logically and practically it includes the apprehension of these purposes, but it does not include their initiation or modification. We have attempted to demonstrate how it is possible to distinguish between administration and over-all policy-making and, thus, to reduce the ambiguity that surrounds the present use of the term "administration."

There is some evidence for the assumption that the term "administration" is applied generally, even if not exclusively, to the activity that we have described. Also it appears that, as organizations become larger, administration becomes more distinguishable as the activity we have described. In educational organizations, at present, it is not always clearly distinguished in the public and professional mind from the other functions of the organization, although it is obviously on the way to such recognition. At present, administration is in a transitional stage; it is emerging as an entity in its own right, but it is still often confused with other activities. Thus the ambiguous status of the educational administrator. Both he and the public are confused by the dual nature of his role as administrator and teacher or expert in education. He is regarded as a symbol of organization, of organization striving to maintain its internal equilibrium and to survive in a system of competing organizations, and he is also regarded as a symbol of the professional education activity. As his position changes from that of head teacher or chief academician to that of administrator, he will become recognized more and more as the person who performs the functions we have described, and his responsibilities will not differ essentially from those of administrators in other organizations.

This prophecy will doubtless be anathema to many educational administrators. Nearly all of them have been teachers; understandingly and laudably they are reluctant to relinquish the role of teacher, academician, or school man. Furthermore, it is probably rather chilling to them, as well as to others, to contemplate the rise of a managerial class in education, administrators of devastating sameness, without academic profile, that are interchangeable with administrators in all organizations. However, even a cursory observation of the facts makes the prophecy plausible. The demands of the modern school organization compel the almost complete devotion of the administrator to duties that we have labeled administrative.[19] Buildings, budgets, buses, and bonds consume his time and energy. Vestiges of his earlier role as principal teacher remain, but the more intimately the public are acquainted with the school administrator's work, the more likely

[19] See Jean Howerton's "School Superintendents Are Too Busy to Act as Educators," *Louisville Courier-Journal*, March 17, 1957, Sect. 4, p. 1.

it is that it will be viewed as purely managerial. In a revealing answer to a query, a local school board member told the author that he regarded the local superintendent as primarily an administrator, but that he usually thought of the superintendent of the intermediate district as primarily a specialist in education.

In company with executives of other organizations, school administrators seem to have a great deal in common with them; both are known to be concerned about personnel, public relations, building construction, and the interest rates on municipal bonds. Also, they are usually able to converse about these matters with a sophistication that is remarkable in school men. At the same time, they may be addressed as "Professor" or "Doctor" and they are surrounded with a faint aura of the academic world. In appearance, however, they generally reflect the world of administration rather than the groves of academe.

The current ambiguous status of the administrator in education and his departure from the prototype of chief academician are recognized in frank discussions among members of the craft:

> No one has ever sharply defined the role of the superintendent. There was a day, not too long ago, when the head supervisor, or superintendent, was a learned scholar with perhaps the only professional training among a staff of young high school graduates and poor maiden relations. . . .[20]

But with the increase of the duties and responsibilities which we have defined as administrative

> [The scholar-administrator] turned his attention to raising the dough to pay the teachers and principals and supervisors and coaches and librarians and nurses and custodians and secretaries and bus drivers and cooks. [He] took off his black string tie and shiny blue serge, put on a fetching smile, and shook the taxpayers hand.
>
> There used to be a suspicion that the old boy was a sort of genteel, cultured scholar. I won't say there are no such cultured

---

[20] Charles H. Wilson, A *Teacher Is a Person* (New York: Henry Holt & Company, 1956), p. 277.

gentlemen among us today. But, if there are, they result from fortunate breeding or a passionate hobby. Most of us are pseudo-scholars, politicians, tax experts, public speakers, Rotarians, socialites, engineers, Boy Scouts.[21]

The ambiguity of the administrative function in its present stage prevails in other organizations that are similar in their intrinsic functions to education; e.g., art museums, research foundations, and hospitals, although in the latter administration is more likely to be recognized as being quite distinct from professional medicine. The relationship between administration and professionalism will be discussed later; here we merely intend to point out that the professional or the expert who assumes an administrative position in an organization, the intrinsic function of which is his specialty, immediately takes on an ambiguous role. The position demands administration; the expert expects to continue his status as a professional in his field. In art museums, for example, the directors still regard themselves as art experts, historians, critics, or connoisseurs, but the position demands a full-time manager. Commenting on the resignation of a museum director, a leading art journal editorialized as follows:

> Francis Taylor's is actually one more, and a very significant one, of a mounting series of active groans over the bureaucratic burdens that threaten to swamp our trained scholars who become operative as administrators as well as savants, in their own specialized fields—whether as museum directors, college presidents, even heads of atomic research laboratories.[22]

Two other examples outside education will indicate that in an organization of savants, the administrative role is emerging as something distinct from the intrinsic functions of the organization. The Chief Justice of the Supreme Court has been selected in recent years for abilities other than his sheer brilliance in the law. Although this position can hardly be designated as purely administrative, it does have a great many responsibilities of that

[21] *Ibid.*
[22] Editorial in *Art News*, January, 1955, p. 15.

kind. In an entirely different kind of organization—the Advanced Research Project Agency for the Department of Defense—the appointment of a director provides an even more striking example. A vice-president of a large industrial concern was appointed, and his duties were described as "organization, the handling of scientists, and the clear establishment of lines of authority." [23]

Turning again to educational administration, we find that it is not teaching or scholary abilities that are paramount in the selection of principals and school superintendents. Notwithstanding the frequent lament that the best teachers are taken out of the classrooms for administrative work, it seems likely that, rather than the most learned or the most intellectual, the teachers with the most generally desirable personal characteristics are selected for administrative positions. The qualities desired may be good appearance, the ability to get along with people, interest in community affairs, and conformity in dress, manners, and ideas. These traits may be associated with good teaching or they may not; but, if they are, they are not peculiar to the teacher. It appears likely that a person with a theoretical turn of mind, or highly specialized intellectual interests, would not be considered good administrative material. Some exceptions may be found at the college and university level, but even there the savant may be at a disadvantage.

Originality and creativity, as well as conventional competence in intellectual matters, are not likely to be considered particularly desirable in educational administrators. It is true that in business the stereotype of the successful administrator contains some elements of ingenuity and boldness; but if there is a real difference between business administrators and educational administrators in this regard, it may be attributed to the fact that: (1) education is a more conservative enterprise than business; or (2) there is a strong entrepreneurial tradition in business. However, if the thesis

[23] New York *Herald-Tribune*, February 8, 1958, p. 1.

The Administrative Process

of the organization man [24] is correct, the modern business administrator conforms to the pattern that we contend is common to educational administration—the safe, prudent, practical man who exemplifies stability.

Systematic studies of how the public regards the nature and function of administration in education are few indeed, but those we have would indicate that our theory is correct. Well-defined characterizations of school administrators in popular and nonprofessional literature are difficult to find. The teacher has been portrayed in literature, and often not very flatteringly [25]—a few colorful headmasters, rarely a public school principal, and even more infrequently a school superintendent. Judged by the number of articles in popular magazines devoted to administration, this aspect of education is much less popular than curriculum, teaching, students, methods, and the aims of education.[26] Studies of newspaper editorials on education indicate that administrative matters rank very high in frequency of mention, but that public school administrators do not.[27] The conclusion of one study is that

> ... administrators as a group fail to impress their leadership on the social scene. We are left with the feeling that the absence of much editorial comment on them may perhaps arise, after all, from their failure to be as instrumental, as useful, as consequential as they could have been.[28]

[24] William H. Whyte, Jr., *The Organization Man* (New York: Simon and Schuster, 1956).
[25] Don Charles, "Stereotypes of the Teacher in American Literature," *Educational Forum*, XIV (March, 1950), 299–304.
[26] John Walton, "Major Emphases in Education in a Selected List of Annual Periodicals, 1928–1947," unpublished doctoral dissertation, The Johns Hopkins University, Baltimore, Maryland, p. 101.
[27] Rhodes R. Stanley, *Newspaper Editorials on American Educators* (Philadelphia: University of Pennsylvania, 1941); and Charles R. Foster, Jr., *Editorial Treatment of Education in the American Press*, Harvard Bulletin in Education, No. 21 (Cambridge, Mass.: Harvard University, 1938).
[28] Foster, *Editorial Treatment of Education* . . . , p. 103.

Our conclusion is that administration is considered as an extremely important matter—thus the high frequency of newspaper editorials on the subject—but that the administrator is not a colorful figure engaged in innovations. The "argument from silence" would indicate that this is true.

CHAPTER IV

the Discernment of purpose

ACCORDING TO our definition and analysis of educational administration, its three principal functions are: (1) the discernment or apprehension of an organization's purposes; (2) the direction of activities within an educational organization in their reciprocal relations toward the accomplishment of accepted purposes; and (3) the providing of means for an organization's survival. Of these three functions, the discernment of purpose logically comes first, although in practice the temporal relations are often difficult to distinguish. In this chapter, we shall attempt to determine how the purposes of educational organizations are formulated and to suggest methods whereby the educational administrator may find out what they are, how they change, and their hierarchical order.

How the Purposes of Education Are Determined

Even a cursory examination of the structure and functioning of education in the United States reveals at once the presence of many formal purpose, or over-all policy-making, agencies. It also reveals a great deal of concern over the years about where this purpose-making power will reside. That so homely and child-loving an activity as education should be the cause of dissension, and that statesmen, politicians, and ecclesiastics, as well as parents and teachers, are sensitive about the control of educational policy may seem rather strange; however, they all have faith, whether it is warranted or not, in the power of education to develop attitudes, values, and loyalties. In this country most, although not all, elementary and secondary school organizations derive their over-all policies largely from local and state governments, and particularly from the somewhat autonomous school government at both levels. As a special form of public administration, educational administration must respond to diffuse and different public policy-making agencies. This situation demands rather complicated mechanisms for detecting changes in purpose. We shall now attempt to trace the lines and filaments through which these changes are registered.

The general purposes of public educational organizations are given formal expression by (1) state constitutions, statutory enactments, by-laws of state boards, and adjudication by state courts and state educational authorities; (2) local boards of education; and (3) national legislation and federal courts. We shall discuss briefly the policy-making functions of these agencies in the order in which they appear.

Public education in the United States is legally a function of the several states. Since the powers of the government of the United States are delegated rather than inherent, and since the Constitution makes no mention of education, any positive power that the federal government may possess in educational matters must arise from some implied grant of authority. On the other hand, because of the Tenth Amendment ("The powers not delegated to the United States by the Constitution, nor prohibited by it to the states, are reserved to the states respectively, or to the people"), the courts have formulated a principle that education

The Discernment of Purpose

is a state function. As a matter of fact, there is no clearer principle in the law:

> . . . it is obvious that, subject to constitutional limitations, the state legislature has plenary power with respect to matters of educational policy. In the absence of constitutional limitations, the ends to be attained and the means to be employed are wholly subject to legislative determination. The legislature may determine the types of schools to be established throughout the state, the means of their support, the organs of their administration, the content of their curricula, and the qualifications of their teachers.[1]

All states have constitutional provisions for education. The provisions tend to be general in nature, requiring the legislatures to maintain a system of free, public, nonsectarian education. For example, the constitution of the State of Maryland provides the following:

Declaration of Rights

Art. 43. That the Legislature ought to encourage the diffusion of knowledge and virtue, the extension of a judicious system of general education, the promotion of literature, the arts, sciences, agriculture, commerce and manufactures, and the general amelioration of the condition of the people.

Constitution

Article VIII, Education

Section 1. The General Assembly, at its first session after the adoption of this Constitution, shall, by law, establish throughout the State a thorough and efficient system of free Public Schools; and shall provide by taxation or otherwise, for their maintenance.

Section 2. The System of Public Schools, as now constituted, shall remain in force until the end of the first session of the General Assembly, and shall then expire, except so far as adopted or continued by the General Assembly.

---

[1] Newton D. Edwards, *The Courts and the Public Schools* (Chicago: University of Chicago Press, 1955), pp. 27–28.

Section 3. The School Fund of the State shall be kept inviolate, and appropriated only to the purposes of education.[2]

In addition to the general provisions for education, the constitutions of twenty states explicitly provide for the creation, method of selection of members, and duties of one or more governing boards for their state institutions of higher education. Although it is a historic principle that a legislature may not delegate its legislative powers to any other tribunal, agency, or official, it may in the carrying out of its policies create administrative boards and confer upon them broad discretionary powers, so broad, as a matter of fact, that it is difficult often to distinguish one power from the other. Thus, in the creation of state boards for education, teacher education, vocational education, universities, and agricultural colleges, the legislature would appear to have delegated its legislative powers. For example, the public school laws of Maryland provide that "They [the State Board of Education] shall determine the educational policies of the State; they shall enact by-laws for the administration of the public school system, which when enacted and published shall have the force of law." [3]

However, the act creating the administrative board theoretically must contain in it some reasonably clear standard by which the discretionary acts of the board are to be governed.[4] In the case of the Maryland State Board of Education, the legislature has enumerated in subsequent sections of the act the duties of the Board, and has added: "The State board of education shall perform such other duties as are assigned to them elsewhere in

[2] *The Public School Laws of Maryland*, Maryland State Department of Education (Baltimore, 1955), pp. v–vi. See John Mathiason Matzen, *State Constitutional Provisions for Education* (New York: Bureau of Publications, Teachers College, Columbia University, 1931).
[3] *The Public School Laws of Maryland*, p. 13.
[4] Edwards, *The Courts and the Public Schools*, pp. 30–31. For a discussion of this principle, see Kenneth Culp Davis, *Administrative Law* (St. Paul, Minn.: West Publishing Company, 1951), pp. 41–88.

The Discernment of Purpose

this Article, or may be assigned to them from time to time by the General Assembly.[5]

Obviously these agencies determine, or can determine within the legislative limits, over-all policy for public education. The question may arise: What is their responsibility for private education? While the extent of state control over private schools and colleges is not yet clearly established, these principles seem to hold: (1) the state may not prohibit private schools; (2) it may not prohibit the teaching of certain well-recognized subjects in private schools; (3) it may prohibit any kind of educational activity that threatens the public safety or is subversive of public works or the public welfare; and (4) it may prescribe some academic standards for private schools.[6]

In some states, Pennsylvania, for example, the state laws make rather specific provisions for the curriculum in private or independent schools. In a large measure, however, the purposes of private, parochial, and independent schools are determined by the proprietors, the boards of control, or the supporting churches.

Returning now to public education, we find that, in addition to state constitutional provisions and legislative enactments, state boards of education and chief state school officers, both administrative in their functions at the state level, have allegedly been determiners of over-all policy for local educational organizations. Presumably they have found implied purposes in the formal, legal provisions for education, but they have exerted considerable influence beyond that specified by statutes.[7] It is questionable as to how much chief state school officers generally have modified the over-all policies for education.

A second source of policy for the educational organizations is the local school board. In several respects its status is ambiguous.

[5] *The Public School Laws of Maryland*, p. 23.
[6] Edwards, *The Courts and the Public Schools*, pp. 42–46.
[7] Lee M. Thurston and William H. Roe, *State School Administration* (New York: Harper & Brothers, 1957), Chaps. ii, iii, iv, and v.

We may ask, Is it a part of the school organization or is it extra-organization? Is it a corporation created to carry out a local government function or is it a quasi-corporation created to carry out a state function? And is it an administrative agency exclusively or does it possess legislative powers for education? Technically, according to our theory, the local board of education, when acting in the capacity of formulating over-all policy for the schools is extra-organization as far as the local school system is concerned; and when it engages in the actual operation of the schools, which it seems to be doing less frequently than formerly, it is intra-organization. Technically, also, it is usually a quasi-corporation created to carry out a state function, although its members are usually elected or appointed locally. And as an administrative agency of the state with broad discretionary powers, it performs a dual governmental function: (1) it carries out state policies for education as specified by constitutions, statutes, and by laws; and (2) it acts as a policy-making body for education in the community and is, in effect, a legislative body for education.[8] Since in this country we have a strong tradition of local control, the second function is probably an important activity of most school boards, although because of its administrative nature, the school board may be less bold in initiating policy than it would otherwise be:

> No other public activity is so closely identified with local mores. Interest in the schools is not unusual, and it is an interest that directly involves not only the taxpayer but his family, and therefore his emotions. Those who are indifferent to all other community affairs tend to take a proprietary interest in the schools their children attend, or have attended. State influence in public education has grown in recent years in proportion to state aid,[9] but state policies rarely are so important

[8] See American Association of School Administrators, Thirty-fourth Yearbook, *School Board-Superintendent Relationships* (Washington, D.C., 1956); also, Willard B. Spalding, "The School Board as Policy-Making Body," in *Improving Public Education Through School Board Action* (Pittsburgh: University of Pittsburgh Press, 1950).

[9] An investigation by Robert D. Fleisher, "The Development of the Relationship of Legal Fiscal Controls to the Extent of State Aid for Education as Ap-

as local forces in the shaping of educational policies and practices.[10]

Insofar as policy-making for education is concerned, it is the broad, so-called discretionary powers of school boards that are significant.[11] Because the board acts in both an executive and quasi-legislative capacity, it is not always easy to distinguish when it is operating as an administrative agency for the general state school organization and when it is acting as an extraorganization policy-making body for the local schools. The complications of organizations within organizations have been considered in an earlier chapter and will be returned to later; for the moment, it is sufficient to point out that school boards have policy-making responsibilities that they cannot delegate:

> There are many matters which the board cannot and should not delegate to the administrative officers, however. These include *major changes in school policies,* the approval of major extensions or reductions in school curricula, the approval of building and construction programs, basic changes in school organization, the review and approval of school budgets, approval of major contracts, exercise of the taxing and borrowing authority of the school city, and general review of school operations as circumstances may indicate or require.[12]

The American school board, as a form of local government, deserves serious study. The government of private and independent educational institutions, existing as it does under charters or other forms of franchise, has been referred to as "shadow" government;

---
plied to Pennsylvania, 1921–1953," *Journal of Educational Research,* 1 (October, 1956), 81–90, does not support this view.

[10] Henry Ashmore, *The Negro and the Public Schools* (Chapel Hill, N.C.: University of North Carolina Press, 1954), p. 82.

[11] See John D. Massick, *The Discretionary Power of School Boards* (Durham, N.C.: Duke University Press, 1949).

[12] *The Public School System of Gary, Indiana* (Chicago: Public Administration Service, 1955), p. 25; italics added. For a brief, but good, summary of the status of the school board, see Calvin Grieder and William Everett Rosenstengel, *Public School Administration* (New York: The Ronald Press Company, 1954), Chap. v.

but public school boards are governmental in the fullest sense. Representing, so far as the state is concerned, administration, they continue to perform a local, policy-making function for education, which in theory they derive from statutes, but, which may well represent vestigial local legislation for public education.

The third major source of official policy for the schools is the federal government. Notwithstanding the fact that education is a state function, the national government from the days of the Continental Congress to the National Defense Education Act have legislated for education. Furthermore, the Supreme Court of the United States has obliquely determined policies for the schools. By the Judiciary Act of 1789, any statute or any authority under state government became subject to review in the federal courts in order to determine whether or not it was "repugnant" to the Constitution. The Supreme Court has ruled on the constitutionality of school laws and practices, more frequently in recent years than in former, and particularly on those laws and procedures that impaired contractual relations or violated the ambiguous "due process of law." [13]

These, then, are the legal and formal agencies for the determination of the over-all policies or purposes for education. The state constitutions include provisions, the state legislatures enact laws, the state boards pass rules and by-laws, the courts decide the constitutionality of laws and the legality of acts, and the local school boards in frequent sessions change purposes. It should be mentioned again that the school boards at all levels also act in an administrative capacity. But all these formal agencies with their laws, decisions, and clearly enunciated policies provide a thin and fragile barrier to the direct influence of the people on their

---

[13] For the extent to which the Supreme Court has influenced educational policy, see Edwards *The Courts and the Public Schools*, pp. 1–22; Clark Spurlock, *Education and the Supreme Court* (Urbana, Ill.: University of Illinois Press, 1955); Harry Pratt Judson, *Our Federal Republic* (New York: The Macmillan Company, 1925), Chap. VIII; and Edward S. Corwin, "The Supreme Court as National School Board," *Law and Contemporary Problems*, LIV, No. 1 (Winter, 1949), 3–22.

The Discernment of Purpose

schools. Education appears to be more sensitive to the will of the people, directly and without an intermediary, than any other public enterprise. Leys, who recognized the great area of discretion in the administration of service agencies, apparently saw this fact as evidence that the administrators determined the over-all policies of their organizations:

> Under the complex conditions of our industrial society those who enforce the laws must make at least part of the laws they enforce. We can no longer pretend that executives merely fill gaps that have inadvertently been left in statute and constitution. Legislators admit that they can do little more with such subjects as factory sanitation, international relations, and public education than to lay down a general public policy within which administrators will make detailed rules and plans of action.[14]

Rather than assuming that the gap is filled by "administrative discretion" in the sense of adding to or changing over-all policies, we believe that there is continuously operating upon the public school administrator a popular will both vocal and taciturn to which he conforms in his decisions about educational purposes. It would be interesting to know whether or not, when administration is not so subject to immediate popular control, the legislation for the purposes of public agencies is more detailed and specific; and whether or not the great area of administrative discretion that is permitted educational administrators is considered safe because of the immediate control of public opinion. Our theory holds that the educational administrator must discern, interpret, and, often, translate into specific objectives for the schools that residue of educational purposes that is not expressed in formal policies (some of them are never so expressed) but which exists in the popular will. Here, admittedly, our theory faces a severe test, and one comparable to that placed before it by the sinuous relations between ends and means; for in attempting or pretending to discern the purposes for the educational organization as they exist in the

[14] Wayne A. R. Leys, "Ethics and Administrative Discretion," *Public Administration Review*, III, No. 1 (Winter, 1943), 10.

popular or community will, the administrator has an opportunity to introduce his own ideas about what the purposes of education should be.

Reasonable questions of the kind that will inevitably be raised here must be anticipated. We propose to answer them by stating first that, in general, administrators appear to be selected for their ability to discern and to conform to the community will for education, and second that administrators who do not do so are unsuccessful, i.e., are unable to carry out their objectives or lose their jobs. It should be pointed out here that when the administrator's personal views, no matter how original or intense, coincide with the purposes of education held by the policy-making bodies or the latent will of the public, there is no administrative imposition.

Now there are obvious exceptions and discrepancies to our theory that must be taken into account. In addition to the "foolish servant" aspiring to the role of statesman and law-maker, and the anachronistic entrepreneur in education, we may have five conditions under which these exceptions may appear to be true: (1) the activities of the educational administrator as professional consultant to the board of education; (2) the confusion between policies about operational matters and organizational purposes; (3) organizations operating within organizations; (4) administrators acting as pawns of special interest groups; and (5) the somewhat ambiguous role of the college and university president.

Under the first set of conditions, the apparent exceptions occur because boards of education have come to rely heavily and often somewhat uneasily upon the school superintendent for advice in technical and professional matters, a practice that has been interpreted to mean that the administrator determines over-all policies. The public school laws of Maryland, for example, require that "the county board of education, subject to the provisions of this Article, the by-laws, courses of study and policies of the state board of education, shall prescribe, on the written recommendation of the county superintendent, courses of study for the schools

The Discernment of Purpose

under their jurisdiction. . . ."[15] Here it is obvious that the county superintendent's recommendations must be subject to the policies of the state board of education, but in practice it may appear to the observer that the county superintendent is actually imposing his own policies on the county board.

An example of the second class of apparent exceptions may be taken from the survey of the Gary, Indiana, public schools, which was cited above:

> As currently organized, the School City of Gary functions at two major levels of activity. The first is the policy level and involves the Board of School Trustees, the superintendent of schools and two assistant superintendents, one for business and the other for educational administration. The second level is the operational level and involves the superintendent, the assistant superintendents, the principals, and all other supervisory and administrative officials in charge of various aspects of the school program. It also includes the very sizeable number of committees—composed of administrative and teaching personnel—that participate in the formulation of policies for operational phases of school activity.[16]

We have already seen from the same survey that the school board could not delegate to any administrative officers the responsibility for any "major changes in school policies, the approval of major extensions or reductions in school curricula," [17] but the Policy Manual of the Board of School Trustees specifies that the superintendent "shall have responsibility for the formulation and recommendation of school policies, procedures, and programs to the board of school trustees. . . ." Here the word "policies" may refer to procedures, but if it does refer to over-all policies or purposes, we may argue that they are not necessarily the superintendent's own views, and that in any event they must be accepted by the Board of School Trustees.

The third class of apparent exceptions arises from the fact that

---
[15] *The Public School Laws of Maryland*, 1955, No. 1, pp. 52–53.
[16] *The Public School System of Gary, Indiana*, p. 21.
[17] *Ibid.*, p. 25.

organizations exist within organizations. This subordination of organizations tends to limit their purposes, and what may be the purposes of the subordinate organization may be simply the means of the more inclusive organization. While clear examples of this type are probably less easily found in education than in industry, we may regard the state board of education as an organization for carrying out state educational policies, on the one hand, and for determining through its by-laws and regulations some of the purposes for smaller educational organizations, on the other. The fact that the state board represents a much less tightly structured organization than the local school systems should not obscure the fact that it is an organization with certain well-defined purposes, one of which is the determination of policy for smaller units of the educational system. This purpose it did not formulate for itself, but, rather, obtained it from a still more inclusive organization, the state government.

Perhaps to refer to our fourth category as *apparent* exceptions is somewhat erroneous, because exceptions to our theory undoubtedly do occur, when educational administrators, acting as pawns for special interest groups, attempt to circumvent or to influence the over-all policy-making agencies. Many pressure groups seeking to control the policies for education apparently seek out the administrators as their agents. This fact may be taken as evidence that the administrator is largely responsible for determining policy; however, the pressure groups may be mistaken. Moreover, the evidence is not clear that the more sophisticated pressure groups rely on the administrator nearly as much as they do legislatures and boards of education. But there is no gainsaying the fact that some groups with a mission attempt to indoctrinate administrators with the hope that they will influence the over-all policies of the educational system. While this activity may be due in large measure to a general evangelistic zeal that seeks to convince anyone who is accessible, there are those who believe that the administrator occupies a strategic position for the modification of educational purposes. It would be interesting to see how many of such groups also believe that the administrator should determine

The Discernment of Purpose

over-all policies; it would be even more interesting to find out just how successful administrators can be in imposing their own views when they conflict with those of the policy-making bodies that we have described above.

A special group of educational administrators—college and university presidents—furnishes what appears to be the most cogent evidence against our theory that educational administrators have little to do with major policy changes. Enormous documentation can be produced, and would indeed be regarded as a work of supererogation, to prove that college and university presidents have been extremely influential in determining and changing the purposes of higher education. One has only to think of Gilman of Hopkins, Eliot of Harvard, and Harper of Chicago to suspect some fallacy in the theory that has been presented. We are forced to account for this negative evidence.

In attempting to account for this apparent exception, we are justified in saying, first, that the college presidency is a unique position in administration. The species flourishes almost exclusively in the United States. While one of the principal functions of the office has always been one that we recognize as administrative, many other duties have been associated with it. "A president should be a scholar, teacher, organizer, authority on education, administrator, financier, writer, orator, judge of men, leader, inspirer of youth, publicist, diplomatist, man of the world, moral idealist." [18]

We must admit that, in addition to performing those duties that we call administrative, college and university presidents have engaged in the intrinsic functions of the organization, i.e., teaching and research, and they have definitely determined over-all policy. The trend, however, has been toward the full-time administrator.[19] The administration of colleges and universities has become so complex that the chief administrative officer expends

[18] Margaret Farrand Thorp, *Neilson of Smith* (New York: Oxford University Press, 1956), pp. 4–5.
[19] Charles Franklin Thwing, *The College President* (New York: The Macmillan Company, 1926). More studies are needed. Cf. Father John Colman's unpublished master's thesis on the history of the Presidency, St. John's University, Brooklyn, The Johns Hopkins University, Baltimore, 1956.

his time and energy in problems of public relations, finance, coordination, and other purely administrative duties; in the words of a perceptive president of long experience, he has become a man of Management rather than a man of Learning.[20] However, more pertinent to this part of our theory are this president's views on policy. On the one hand he says, "The most important qualification that a college president can bring to his job is a philosophy of education";[21] but he goes on to specify what this philosophy should be: "a faith in education as salvation; the doctrine of national necessity; the acceptance of utility; and views on education and democracy."[22] Clearly, he is stating in general terms the current national and community purposes of higher education.

Perhaps, however, we should not accept too quickly the theory that presidents have, on the whole, deviated from the administrative role as we have defined it. A history of the college presidency in the United States might reveal that comparatively few college presidents have actually been influential in changing the course of education—except when they were the founders of institutions. Because they have stood out so as founders, they are the presidents who have been remembered. Also, it should be noted that college presidents have stood as symbols for their institutions; colleges have depended upon their zeal, their color, their idiosyncrasies for support and survival. These more spectacular activities, therefore, may be classified as administrative, although they may have been interpreted in many instances as determiners of policy and purpose.

The doctrine that the educational administrator is not the determiner of educational purposes may be uncongenial to some. But to assume that he is, appears to be both illogical and empirically false. The origin of the idea that he is, probably lies in the tradition of a few school administrators who were innovators and statesmen. To suggest to every educational administrator, burdened with the enormous responsibility of accomplishing edu-

---

[20] Harold W. Stoke, *The American College President* (New York: Harper and Brothers, 1959), p. 3.
[21] *Ibid.*, p. 161.
[22] *Ibid.*, p. 170.

The Discernment of Purpose

cational objectives, that he is an educational statesman will give to some few men an exaggerated sense of their importance; for the majority it will tend to increase their anxiety because they realize the futility of such attempts.[23] It is a rare individual who can be both an effective administrator and a determiner of purposes; and the occasions for the latter are rare. Although there is uncertainty about the purposes of education today, the people and the policy-making agencies resent the intrusion of any professional or administrative group. In the last analysis, decisions about what should be done by the schools are lay decisions; neither the expert in administration nor the scholar has demonstrated any superiority over the layman in judgments about the purposes of education.

But why not strive for the "administrator-statesman" in education? We have had statesmen in the past who have profoundly influenced the course of education; there is obviously a need for statesmanship today. In the words of Walter Lippmann:

> There are many things which people cannot understand until they have lived with them for a while. Often, therefore, the great statesman is bound to act boldly in advance of his constituents. When he does this he states his judgment as to what the people will in the end find to be good against what the people happen ardently to desire. This capacity to act upon the hidden realities of a situation in spite of appearance is the essence of statesmanship. It consists in giving the people not what they want but what they will learn to want.[24]

Now if this is a good definition of statesmanship, we can readily foresee the grave consequences if every administrator presumed to give the people "not what they want but what they will learn to want." More comfortable, as well as more realistic, is our doctrine that the administrator has the important responsibility

---

[23] For a similar attempt, see Willard B. Spalding's *The Superintendency of Public Schools—An Anxious Profession* (Cambridge, Mass.: Harvard University Press, 1954), pp. 7–8.
[24] Walter Lippmann, *A Preface to Morals* (New York: The Macmillan Company, 1929), p. 282.

of carrying out the objectives of educational organizations. However, he must know what these objectives are and interpret them with fidelity.

Methods of Discernment

Whatever prestige and importance we have taken away from the average educational administrator by denying him membership in the councils of statesmen who change the course of educational policy, we shall now repay by indicating the importance of the discernment of educational purposes and the kind and level of ability required. This responsibility in administration requires an unusual sensitivity and a patience that is rare. The prudence and practical wisdom of administration waits upon a clear vision of the ends to be achieved, and this vision is attained through infinite patience and imperturbable graciousness in encouraging the expression of the popular will. In addition to the honest and accurate reading of the expressed purposes, the administrator must often preside over the prolonged labors attending the birth of new goals and purposes for the educational organization.

In some organizations the ends are clear, undisputed, and relatively stable; their discernment is a simple matter. In educational organizations there are some purposes that are definite and perennial—the achievement of literacy, for example, but there are others that are obscure, intangible, changing, and controversial, such as the teaching of spiritual values. In a social order afflicted with accelerated change, institutions display concern about their purposes; some purposes are decaying, others are emerging, and often they are difficult to distinguish. Because of the peculiar and paradoxical nature of the educational function, at the same time conservative and progressive, its purposes are both modest and ambitious. As the sole custodian of many values and inheritances, the school must bear the calumny of the cultural lag.

The Discernment of Purpose

At the same time, if the school abandoned the purposes with which it, and it alone, is entrusted, it would ultimately be condemned.

The current unrest about education undoubtedly stems in part from the fact that the people fear that the basic purposes of the schools are being neglected or supplanted by spurious ones; and there is probably great wisdom in these conservative attitudes toward education. The elimination of Latin from the curriculum, for instance, while apparently a timely and, except for a few vested interests, unimportant action, is in reality a bold move; for if it is removed from the curriculum, whatever objectives it contributed in the liberal and humane education of the individual will be lost to generations. Perhaps Latin should be abandoned entirely, perhaps it should be retained on a very limited scale, or perhaps it should regain some of its former status. It is not the point of this discussion to argue the merits of Latin; rather, it is to point out the awesome irrevocability of what appears to be a simple and obviously unimportant change in purposes of the educational organization.

On the other hand, to employ a wearisome and somniferous cliché, the school as a social institution must meet some of the emerging needs of a society undergoing radical change. To the schools goes some of the responsibility for vocational training, the development of technical skills, the enhancement of moral and spiritual values, and the changing of social attitudes. The administrator must discern the changes in the purposes of education, neither too haltingly, nor too superficially. Fortunately, he enters the school organization aware of a core of purposes and values that are clear, and which he has probably already accepted. In the light of these he makes the majority of his decisions, but he is required to read from many sources in order to discern their nuances, hierarchical positions, and fluctuations.

We have already indicated the formal expressions of educational policy—the constitutions, statutory provisions, by-laws, judicial decisions, and administrative codes. However, because of the ambiguities of legislation, the school superintendent, like all public administrators, is forced to seek for the intent of the laws and regulations. This search is likely to prove chimerical if he spends his time reading the committee hearings and reports, which are likely to be more ambiguous and more confusing than the legislation. Also, the legislation may be purposely vague so that the law may be applied with administrative discretion. The decisions of the courts in educational matters are often a better source of the law's intent than the laws themselves;[25] but these decisions are pertinent to only those laws that the courts have been required to apply to specific cases. They do not extend to that vast area of school practices that have never been subjected to judicial review. In addition to permitting wide latitude in the selection of means, administrative discretion carries with it the responsibility of detecting first hand what the public wants the schools to do.

Extremely crucial for our theory again is this matter of administrative discretion. The purpose decisions that must be made under vague legal and formal provisions, and the residue of such decisions that can find only general and remote sanction, have often been regarded as an administrative prerogative for a number of reasons: (1) by default; (2) administrative responsibility for knowing how policy can be executed presupposes considerable say about what should be done; and (3) as a professional educator the administrator is well-equipped to make decisions about what the purposes of education should be. Even when such a condition has been regarded as undesirable, it has been considered inevitable; the administrator will, openly or clandestinely, consciously or unconsciously, introduce his own purposes for education. For example, the law cannot specify the individuals that are to be employed as teachers. By recommending for employment individuals who possess certain traits, attitudes, and beliefs, the administrator may change the fundamental purposes of an organiza-

[25] *The Corpus Juris Secundum*, Vols. LXXVIII and LXXIX (Brooklyn, N. Y.: American Law Book Company, 1952), contains the body of case law on education.

The Discernment of Purpose

tion in the direction that he desires. That this practice often occurs cannot be denied, but it may also contribute to the failure of the administrator.

The fact of administrative discretion imposes on the administrator the responsibility of supplementing the explicit expressions of educational purpose with an understanding of the community will. With the use of the phrase "community will," we are likely to be charged with a flight into philosophical or social mysticism, or with the introduction of a meaningless phrase that cannot be operationally defined. Because of the associations that the phrase has acquired, it will be necessary to define it as accurately as possible.

It is an ancient observation that man lives in communities that have a kind of organic life of their own.[26] The grounds for this belief have been both empirical and intuitive. Wundt in his *Volker Psychologie* conceived of communities as physical entities that behave as though they have minds of their own, and Royce's idea of the universal community, while partaking of some of the ponderosities of German idealism, is soundly based on what he considered empirical fact.[27] This concept of the community mind has often assumed that it is something more and something different from the sum of the individual minds within the group. McDougall postulates such a mind: "It is not because minds have much in common with one another that I speak of the collective mind, but because the group as such is more than the sum of the individuals, has its own life proceeding according to the laws of group life. . . ."[28]

While we have no prejudice against the organism theory and no preference of temperament for the empirical over the mystical, and, in fact, we do not rule out the mystical nature of the community mind and will—a concept that seems to be included in

---

[26] See, for example, Aristotle's *Politics*.

[27] Josiah Royce, *The Problem of Christianity* (New York: The Macmillan Company, 1914).

[28] William McDougall, *The Group Mind* (New York: G. P. Putnam's Sons, 1928), p. 17.

many discussions of the nature of organizations—we suggest that sufficient empirical clues to the character of the community will may be found to avoid assuming for it a completely ineffable nature.

In attempting to discern the community will for education, the administrator can hardly expect it to present a smooth surface. It will be scarred by oppositions. Communities may agree in willing that the educational function be organized and yet disagree about the details of purpose. The community will on educational objectives is a continually changing composite or sum. This will need not be more than the sum of its components; the sum itself is more than the individual wills. Our metaphor may be considered inappropriate in that it is impossible to add conflicting individual wills and, if we could find a common denominator large enough, it would be too large to be of any practical value. We can reply by continuing the metaphor. The community will for education can seldom be expressed in whole numbers; some combination of mixed numbers is necessary. In practice, the administrator may have to eliminate some of the fractions from the addition, but he should always be aware of them, carrying them in the margin as a reminder that they are part of the general will. Two criteria for relegating them to the margin are suggested: first, since organizations overlap somewhat in their purpose, the schools may be able to neglect those functions that other organizations are attempting to perform; and, second, in the case of conflicting purposes, the schools may invoke the will of the majority but be ever mindful of the opposition of the minority. Usually a core of accepted purposes for the school organization can be discerned. Upon this the administrative will may act with vigor. In the areas of conflicting and obscure purpose, the administrative function is to discover, elucidate, and reconcile, not to impose.

Although the phrase "community will" is rarely encountered, the literature on educational administration is replete with references to the school administrator's relations with the community.[29] The complexity of the concepts and values held by the people of a community has been verified,[30] as well as the varying degrees of interest in education.[31] Also, there has been a great deal of concern about public opinion and public relations for education,[32] the latter including the function that we are describing here. But the discernment of purpose apparently has not been set forth discretely as an administrative function.

Without going into detail or being unduly discursive, we shall indicate briefly some of the traits, methods, and techniques that an administrator may employ to discover the will of the community for education. First, there may be in some individuals a kind of intuitive ability to discern what the people want and the order of their preferences. Some individuals appear to have a sensitivity to the values people hold, to the objectives they want for their educational institutions, and the direction in which the public will is moving. Such judgments may be based on innumerable cues that are detected by more delicate mechanisms than the average person has. Whether this ability can be developed or whether it depends upon innate factors is of the utmost importance in the selection and training of administrators, but this is a problem for the psychologist. We are merely assuming here that such a sensitivity exists and that, if it does, it would enhance the effectiveness of the administrator.

Another method, if we may call it that, is prolonged residence in a community. The rate of turnover among local school super-

[29] For a review of the research literature see Roald F. Campbell, "Situational Factors in Educational Administration," in *Administrative Behavior in Education*, Roald F. Campbell and Russell T. Gregg, eds. (New York: Harper & Brothers, 1957), pp. 234–44.

[30] See, for example, Peter H. Rossi, "The Publics of Local Schools," *Research Memorandum*, No. 2 (Cambridge, Mass.: Harvard University, September, 1954).

[31] See John A. Ramseyer, *Factors Affecting Educational Administration* (Columbus, Ohio: College of Education, Ohio State University, 1955).

[32] For a recent text, see Arthur B. Moehlman and James A. von Zwoll, *School Public Relations* (New York: Appleton-Century-Crofts, 1957).

intendents historically has been rapid,[33] and it has been suggested that they have the status of "strangers" in the community.[34] If long-continued familiarity with the community and being an integral part of it are advantageous, then the current practices decrease their effectiveness. However, it should be pointed out that prolonged residence may fix certain erroneous ideas, whereas a newcomer may see evidence at first glance. But again these are matters of conjecture.

Turning now to some of the techniques, which, although still imperfect, are available to the administrator, we find an abundant literature dealing with both the theoretical and the practical aspects of the community survey [35] and the public opinion poll.[36] While both theories and methodologies in this area are controversial, a familiarity with the techniques available and a sophistication in interpreting the results should be of value.

The last technique to which we shall refer is the citizens' com-

[33] H. Thomas James, "Our Itinerant School-Masters," *Administrator's Notebook*, III, No. 6 (February, 1955). There is some evidence now that the administrator is becoming more permanent.

[34] Harry F. Moore, *Nine Help Themselves*, SWCPEA (Austin: University of Texas, 1955).

[35] See, for example, Moehlman and von Zwoll, *School Public Relations*, Chap. IX, pp. 178–96; the Lynds' *Middletown* and Warner's *Yankee City*; August B. Hollingshead "Community Research Development and Present Conditions," *American Sociological Review*, XIII (April, 1948), 136 ff.; Carl C. Taylor, "Techniques of Community Study and Analysis as Applied to Modern Civilized Societies," in *The Science of Man in the World Crisis*, Ralph Linton, ed. (New York: Columbia University Press, 1945), pp. 416–41; and Joseph S. Himes, "Value Analysis in the Theory of Social Problems," *Social Forces*, XXXIII (March, 1955), 259–62.

[36] See, for example, Moehlman and von Zwoll, *School Public Relations*, Chap. II, pp. 26–40; H. H. Remmers, *Introduction to Opinion and Attitude Measurement* (New York: Harper & Brothers, 1954); Norman John Powell, *Anatomy of Public Opinion* (New York: Prentice-Hall, 1951); Bibliography in Bruce Lannes Smith, Harold D. Lasswell, and Ralph D. Casey, *Propaganda, Communication, and Public Opinion* (Princeton, N.J.: Princeton University Press, 1946), pp. 352–61; William Albig, *Public Opinion* (New York: McGraw-Hill Book Company, 1939); and Harold C. Hand, *What People Think About Their Schools* (Yonkers-on-Hudson, New York: World Book Company, 1948).

mittee.[37] These committees may be organized by the administrator or they may be formed in protest to what the schools are doing or failing to do; and, at times, the protests are against procedures rather than policies. In any event, they are a means whereby the administrator may learn the will of the community for education. As a matter of fact, the appearance of citizens' groups as an administrative technique is evidence for our theory.

We have limited the application of this theory largely to the administration of public education, and, although the phrase has not been used, the compulsion to use the words "democratic administration" has been well-nigh irresistible. This method of discerning the purposes of education is, we hope, democratic, but that is not why we have included it. Certainly the sources of over-all policy-making for public education coincide with American democratic and, perhaps, agrarian ideals, but if in other organizations these sources are different and less complex, the principle still applies. In all organizations the discernment of purpose is a major administrative responsibility.[38]

[37] See *Fifty-third Yearbook*, Part I, National Society for the Study of Education, Citizen Cooperation for Better Public Schools (Chicago: University of Chicago Press, 1954); David B. Dreiman, *How to Get Better Schools* (New York: Harper & Brothers, 1956); and *Public Action for Powerful Schools*, Metropolitan School Study Council, Research Studies No. 3 (New York: Bureau of Publications, Teachers College, Columbia University, 1949).

[38] See James D. Thompson and William J. McEwen, "Organizational Goals and Environment: Goal Setting as an Interaction Process," *American Sociological Review*, XXIII, No. 1 (February, 1958), 23–31.

CHAPTER V

Co-ordination

THE GROWTH OF organizations is a contemporary phenomenon of note. In organizations the solitary thinkers have been set, and those thinkers that have not are enormously dependent upon them. This attempt to formulate a theory of educational administration, for example, is a highly individualistic enterprise. Yet in various ways its completion depends upon the activities of many other people working in a university: books, pamphlets, journals, and fugitive materials that a university has ordered, classified, and loaned are essential; colleagues employed by the university will read and criticize the ideas expressed; and in many ways the resources of a university provide the time, the means, and the environment for such an activity.

Now a university, like a school, a church, an army, an industry, an art museum, a government agency, or a hospital, is an organization. A simple definition of organization is that it is a group of two or more people working together for the accomplishment of a common purpose. In its broadest sense the term includes all cooperative efforts, no matter how loosely, informally, or impermanently they are related. Most individuals working in an organization are probably concerned to some degree about the common purpose; "What this university should do" is a familiar preface to conversation in the faculty club. Even in industry, with the highly specialized nature of its activities, most workers are interested in the finished product. It must be admitted, however, that members of many organizations do not join the organization because of their interest in the over-all purpose, but rather because the organization provides for them an opportunity to achieve highly individual goals. Once they become members of an organization it is likely that they will acquire at least a mild interest in the goals of the organization. But the organization cannot depend entirely on the interests of its individual members; someone within the organization must make the attainment of the organizational goals his primary concern.

Although organizations vary greatly in the degree to which they are formally organized, there are many thousands of them that are consciously arranged, fairly discreet, and comparatively permanent. In them the various persons, functions, specialties, and spaces are allocated and directed in their reciprocal relations in such a way that they contribute maximally to the accomplishment of the over-all purpose. "To give things and actions their proper proportions and to adapt the means to the end"[1]—this we call co-ordination. And this is the second of our three administrative functions.

The relations between organization and co-ordination are intimate indeed. The former has been defined as a "system of consciously coordinated activities or forces of two or more persons."[2] Another definition makes them almost synonymous: "This term [co-ordination] expresses the principles of organization in toto."[3] Perhaps it is possible to say that co-ordination, in the

[1] Henri Fayol, "The Administrative Theory in the State," in *Papers on The Science of Administration*, Luther H. Gulick and L. Urwick, eds. (New York: Institute of Public Administration, Columbia University, 1937), p. 103.
[2] Chester I. Barnard, *The Functions of the Executive* (Cambridge, Mass.: Harvard University Press, 1954), p. 73.
[3] James D. Mooney and Alan C. Reiley, *Onward Industry* (New York: Harper & Brothers, 1931), p. 19.

sense that we use the term, is the activity that creates and maintains an organization. So vital is it in the administrative process that we are justified in devoting a great deal of attention to formulating as unambiguous a definition as possible and in examining the conditions necessary for its operation. Such a definition does not presume to dispel all the mystery of its nature; rather its purpose is to render the concept of co-ordination clearly enough to relate it to other concepts that are used in this general theory.

Definition

In the preliminary definition given above, co-ordination is referred to as the activity that allocates and directs the various persons, functions, specialties, and spaces with a view to their reciprocal relations in such a way that they contribute maximally to the accomplishment of an organization's purposes. Implicit in this definition is the admission of personnel. Therefore, we can equate co-ordination somewhat with three functions in the classical theories of administration: staffing, allocating or organizing, and directing. In the performance of each of these three functions the administrator must keep two things in mind: the importance of the specialties for the achievement of the organization's over-all purposes; and their reciprocal relations. We shall now attempt to show how each of these functions meets our definition of co-ordination in an educational organization.

The staffing of the schools is an administrative responsibility. Technically, boards of education employ teachers and other personnel, and in doing this they carry out their legal duties as administrative agents of the state. But usually the superintendent of schools, or a division of his office, has the responsibility for selecting the persons to be employed. In order to make an ap-

Co-ordination

propriate selection, he must have three kinds of information at hand: (1) the purposes of the school system; (2) the specialties that are needed to contribute toward the realization of those purposes; and (3) the qualifications of the applicants. Recognition of this fact is not lacking in the literature on educational administration:

> Before any intelligent decision can be made with respect to a candidate's fitness for a position, the requirements of the job need to be weighed carefully. This implies that consideration be given to the philosophy of the school system and that the duties and functions of the person who is to fill the post be analyzed and clearly set forth. In brief, a clear statement of what is expected should be formulated. If the vacancy to be filled is a classroom teaching job, it is important to inquire whether or not the appointee will be asked to assume guidance responsibilities, to participate in curriculum improvement activities, to work closely with the PTA, to provide leadership for a school community project, or whether his functions will be limited almost exclusively to classroom activities.[4]

Some discrepancies in practice, or counter examples, are apparent when we turn to the staffing of colleges and universities. First, the job analysis approach is probably not so prevalent, and, second, faculties usually have a great deal to say about the persons who are admitted to the organization. The first discrepancy may be explained by the fact that in some colleges and universities their purposes are somewhat less specific than those of the lower levels of education. For example, a graduate school devoted to research might select a person on the basis of his research ability rather that on the basis of his field.

It is not so easy to dispose of the second discrepancy. Perhaps it merely indicates that the professional and technical personnel are the only ones who are deemed capable of passing on the candidate's qualifications. The administration then accepts and

[4] American Association of School Administrators, Thirty-third Yearbook, *Staff Relations in School Administration*, (Washington, D.C., 1955), p. 32.

acts upon their recommendations. This practice occurs in a limited and informal way in some public school systems and in some organizations of other types.

Allocating, the second aspect of co-ordination, has close affinity with what is generally known as "organizing." However, in our definition, it is somewhat more limited than the usual definition of the latter.[5] Here it refers to the arrangement of personnel in relation to function, space, time, and materials in such a way that they can perform their respective work in the organization without mutual interference. In educational organizations, it applies to both teaching and administrative personnel, who must be assigned to units, rooms, and time periods. However trivial it may seem, the assignment of rooms is an important administrative function, and scheduling is of the essence of co-ordination.

The third element in this analysis of the co-ordinating process is directing. Again the essential nature of the process is apparent. Directing the activities within an organization involves knowledge not only of what the activities are, but also of their reciprocal relations. This direction may be tacit or informal, but it is present wherever there is administration. A continuous phase of the co-ordinating function, it has become almost synonymous with the latter. No organization can function without it. In the army and in the schools someone must be able to give directions and to foresee the consequence of acts carried out as a result of that direction for the other personnel and activities within the organization.

Origin

Knowledge of the origin and development of the co-ordinating activity is bound to contribute to our understanding of its nature.

[5] See L. Urwick, "Organization as a Technical Problem," in *Papers on the Science of Administration*.

Co-ordination

Lacking a comprehensive history of administration,[6] we can assume that it arose out of the necessities of organization and that its increase has paralleled the increase in size and complexity of organizations. It is generally true that the increase in the size and complexity of organizations has been responsible for the increase of the co-ordinating function, but there are other possibilities: the impulse to imitate; the desire to pressure an activity for its own sake; and reversed causality, i.e., the growth of the co-ordinating function bringing about larger and more complex organizations. Although the last possibility may appear to be extremely unlikely, it is plausible to assume that progress in the art and science of administration would encourage the growth of organizations. We can be sure that the increasing size and complexity of organizations —whatever the cause—demand more and more efficient co-ordination.

From the not-so-simple one-room school with its teacher-administrator to the present-day complex school organization with its staff of nonteaching administrators, there is a tremendous span of organizational growth. A glance into a medium-sized school system reveals the diversity of personnel and activities that must be co-ordinated: 190 secondary school teachers in 17 different subjects; 328 elementary school teachers in six grades, art, music, and physical education; 81 custodians; 40 principals; 30 clerks and typists; 23 librarians; 11 counselors; 7 secretaries; 4 vice-principals; and one, each, of the following: registrar, social director, dean of girls, dean of boys, head counselor, co-ordinator of pupil personnel services, director of instruction, receptionist, supervisor of child accounting, director of radio education, director of personnel and research, superintendent of operations, superintendent of maintenance, school plant director, and business manager.[7]

To the dimensions of size and number, we should add time

[6] See Albert Lepawsky, *Administration: the Art and Science of Organization and Management* (New York: Alfred A. Knopf, 1949), Chap. IV; and Theodore Lee Reller, *The Development of the City School Superintendency in the United States* (Philadelphia, 1935).

[7] *Public School Directory*, Austin, Texas, 1949–50.

as a factor in increasing the complexity of organizations. Other things being equal, the complexity of an organization, and the consequent need for co-ordination, especially the directing phase, varies directly with the speed of the operations performed. Thus, in an emergency, where speed of performance is essential, activities are more likely to interfere with one another than when the pace is more leisurely. More effective co-ordination is needed in the army under the conditions of war, real or simulated, than in its routine activities. In the educational enterprise, transportation is a much more urgent matter than teaching; and, while in itself it is not so complicated a process as teaching, it adds much more complexity to the organization and requires more co-ordination. This principle may account for the fact that school superintendents and principals often find themselves spending all their time and energy on such matters.

There is no accurate formula that expresses the ratio of the increase in the co-ordinating function to the increase in size and complexity of organizations. Tead has said "As organizations increase in arithmetic size, their difficulties in administrative cohesion grow in geometric proportions"; [8] and Graicunas has attempted to show how the proliferation of relationships as an organization expands is amenable to such a formula.[9] We can, however, submit a corollary to our theory accounting for the growth of co-ordination: the increase in the co-ordinating activity brought on by an increase in the size and complexity of the organization augments the number of activities to be co-ordinated.[10] Thus, if a school administrator creates a position for a curriculum co-ordinator, the position must be staffed, an office assigned, and his activities directed in such a way that they fit into the organiza-

[8] Ordway Tead, *The Art of Administration* (New York: McGraw-Hill Book Company, 1951).
[9] V. A. Graicunas, "Relationship in Organization," in *Papers on the Science of Administration*, pp. 183–87.
[10] See the facetious article in *Fortune*, LIII (March, 1956), 122 ff., entitled "How Seven Employees Can Be Made to do the Work of One"; also, *Parkinson's Law* by C. Northcote Parkinson (Boston: Houghton-Mifflin Company, 1957).

tion. Or, in the words of Parkinson's Law, administrators create work for one another.

It is a truism to assert that society, as the larger, all-inclusive, but less formal organization, has been subject to increasing pressure for greater co-ordination of the activities that are carried on within it. This observation leads to the consideration of whether we shall be able to maintain an open society or whether the pressure for the co-ordination of the various organizations will force a more formally organized one. This pressure accounts for the interests of the political scientist in the matter of co-ordinating the schools, the health department, the public library, the public transportation system, the fire department, and other branches of local public service.[11] The problem of the relation of the schools to other organizations within the larger community organization is back of the argument over fiscally dependent versus independent school districts.[12] Without arguing the merits of the highly co-ordinated versus the more loosely organized community, we can observe here that increasing complexity brings with it a demand for greater co-ordination.

Co-ordination and Democratic Values

Co-ordination is demanded by organization. As will be shown below, it requires certain conditions for its effective operations. These conditions are not always consonant with what may be referred to as democratic values. This situation has developed as follows: Organizations have been created to serve human needs

[11] See Eldon L. Johnson, "Coordination: Viewpoint of a Political Scientist," *The Annals of the American Academy of Political and Social Science*, cccii (November, 1955), 132–42.
[12] See entire issue of *The Annals* referred to in footnote 11, above; also Nelson B. Henry and J. C. Kerwin, *Schools and City Government* (Chicago: The University of Chicago Press, 1938), and J. L. Patrick, "When Is an Independent School Board Independent?" *American School Board Journal*, cxxxii (April, 1956), 27–29.

both individual and social; but organizations have in turn created the need for an activity that may be antithetical to some of the ideals and values of our original democracy. We should be subscribing to something like the "pathetic fallacy" were we to assume that there is some preordained harmony between co-ordination that respects the individual and co-ordination that is effective for an organization. Co-ordination's sole loyalty is to the organization.

How much co-ordination is enhanced by co-operation, "community of interest," and consideration for the individual is not definitely known. Some extremely interesting work that approaches this problem has been done by Halpin, who found that school staffs regarded the effective leader as one who delineates closely the relationship between himself and the group, establishes well-defined patterns of organization, and at the same time reflects friendship and warm human relationships with the group,[13] but he has not attempted to show the relationship between consideration and the achievement of the organization's goals. Probably there is a significant relationship between "co-operative co-ordination" and effectiveness in attaining organizational goals:

> Nevertheless, we must not make the reassuring—but fallacious assumption that this kind of cooperation will always be the most effective means of reaching the organization goal, unless that goal is defined broadly enough to include the values of all participants. This belief in some preordained harmony between administration that respects the individual and administration that is efficient in the usual sense mars the otherwise perceptive writings of Elton Mayo and others of the "Hawthorne Group." [14]

If, as well may be true, effective co-ordination of activities within a complex organization, such as a modern school system, does

[13] Andrew W. Halpin, *The Leadership Behavior of School Superintendents*, School Community Development Study Monograph No. 4 (Columbus: Ohio State University Press, 1956).
[14] Herbert A. Simon, Donald W. Smithburg, and Victor A. Thompson, *Public Administration* (New York: Alfred A. Knopf, 1950), p. 23.

Co-ordination

violence to some of our cherished values, we are not compelled to accept it. We may, however, be under the compulsion to choose between highly effective co-ordination and other values.

Necessary Conditions

Within an organization certain conditions are necessary for the co-ordinating function to operate. These conditions are nonhuman as well as human; there is the need for formal structure as well as for personal qualities in the co-ordinator. We shall now attempt to describe these conditions.

1. STRUCTURE

Much has been written lately about the inappropriateness of the line-and-staff theory of organization for education, and there is a current, untested assumption that educational institutions merely imitated military and industrial organizations in adopting it: "This conception (line and staff) did not arise out of the needs of the (educational organization) but was a copy of the centralized administration developed by the expanding business corporations during the late nineteenth and early twentieth centuries." [15]

The "imitation" hypothesis that is involved to account for the similarity between business and educational organizations is, at first glance, a plausible one, and much more so in this instance than in many others. What is more plausible than to assume that when the educational organization expanded to the point that it needed an elaborate administrative system, it looked to the army and to industry. But however plausible this explanation is, it is not the sole reason, and we do not know that it is the correct

[15] Alfred H. Skogsberg, *Administrative Operational Patterns* (New York: Bureau of Publications, Teachers College, Columbia University, 1950), p. 3.

one. Since the repertory of man's responses to his needs is practically limited, two groups, widely separated, may respond in strangely similar ways to common problems and impulses. If, for example, the early explorers of the Mississippi Valley found that the Indians in that region surrounded their burial places with cromlechs, they could not assume that this practice had been derived from the Welsh, although the frontier rumor of white Indians bolstered this assumption. The cromlech may have been hit upon as a fitting memorial by both the Welsh and the Indians independently of one another.

In the case of two groups or organizations existing in proximity —industry and education in this instance—completely independent adoption of similar organization patterns is less likely to occur, notwithstanding the fact that it probably would if there were not communication between them; one may borrow from the other, not from the desire to imitate, but rather because it finds its neighbor's practice useful. We are handicapped by a lack of historical documentation, but we assume that the exigencies of organization have been the principal cause for the common adaption of line-and-staff structure in both business and education.

However, not all students of the subject have considered the line-and-staff structure inappropriate for educational organizations. Pittenger has deemed it necessary for what he calls "centralized school administrative organization"; he, too, disagrees with the assumption that schools have merely imitated the political, religious, military, and industrial hierarchies in their administrative structure:

> Few of these writers appear to recognize the possibility that the resemblances of which they make so much may be due in considerable part to the fact that the state, the church, the army, industry and the school have all been confronted by a very similar problem; i.e. of coordinating the efforts of a large and varied personnel in order to achieve a single, paramount

objective. Imitation may not have been the sole factor, or even the most important one, in bringing about centralized school administration.[16]

The current objections to the line-and-staff pattern of administrative organization are based largely on the premise that it is undemocratic. This may or may not be the case. The feeling that it somehow is inappropriate for educational organizations may arise from the fact that modern education cherishes democratic values. But, whatever the undesirable consequences, they are the inevitable results of large and complex organizations. Whenever possible these consequences should be avoided, but first of all they should be recognized and admitted.

We shall now attempt to describe briefly the line-and-staff pattern and to justify the historic, albeit rather dogmatic, doctrine that all organizations, including educational, depend upon it for effective co-ordination. In line and staff, the directing function, referred to as "command" in the military organization and bristling with undemocratic overtones, originates with the top administrator and proceeds by way of a well-defined line of authority down through a hierarchy to the last and the lowest personnel working within the organization. The line is the route of the directing and synchronizing process and always runs downward. The staff function is technical and advisory. The staff have the training, the time, and the opportunity to provide the technical knowledge that the administrator needs in order to make his decisions. Urwick has pointed out that the function has not been precisely defined; a staff officer may be a line officer also. If, however, the distinction is clear, the role is as follows, according to Urwick's definition:

> If his relationship to his chief or to this chief's principal subordinates is "purely advisory," co-ordination is essentially an executive function. No part of the executive burden of co-

[16] B. F. Pittenger, "Principles Underlying the Centralized Plan of School Administrative Organization," *The American School Board Journal*, cxvi (April, 1948), 19.

ordination is removed from the chief's shoulders by the receipt of advice, additional to that which he should seek in any event from his principal subordinates. The chief purpose of co-ordination is to secure detailed correlated action by individuals: the chief obstacles it has to overcome are differences of outlook or emphasis leading to heterogeneous imitatives. An official who is only entitled to give advice which may or may not be accepted, cannot relieve this chief of any part of the personal difficulties involved.[17]

The pattern and the procedure are ancient: Julius Caesar, as commanding officer, frequently invited to a council of war his lieutenants, quaestors, tribunes, and centurions of the highest rank. This body could merely advise; the commanding officer was perfectly free to go contrary to its judgment. But when the line officials returned to their posts, they had the authority to carry out the decisions that had been made by their commander.

The comparison of an educational organization to any army will doubtless bring sharp rejoinders. Certainly the sharpness of the line of command is not so clear in the schools, but this difference is due largely to the lack of urgency, for example, the lack of emergency conditions that the army is either preparing for or in which it is immersed. In a major conflagration, race riots, or other crises, the superintendent of schools assumes much the position of a military commander. A schematic representation of the line and staff in its simplest form is given below. It should be remembered that the line officials may be called upon to perform staff functions but that the staff officials do not perform line functions, except insofar as they are responsible for co-ordinating the activities within their own departments. Thus, an assistant superintendent in charge of special classes may be called into council to give advice on technical matters. Then he is acting as a staff official. But when he returns to his place in the administrative studies, he acts as one having authority.

[17] Urwick, "Organization as a Technical Problem," in *Papers on the Science of Administration*, pp. 60–61.

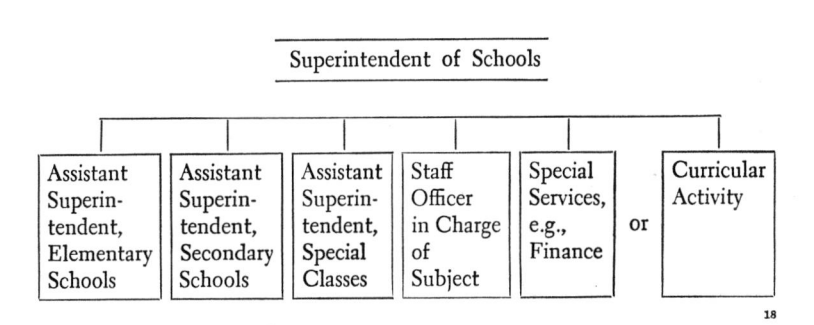

Co-ordination

```
                    ┌─────────────────────────┐
                    │ Superintendent of Schools│
                    └─────────────────────────┘
```

| Assistant Superintendent, Elementary Schools | Assistant Superintendent, Secondary Schools | Assistant Superintendent, Special Classes | Staff Officer in Charge of Subject | Special Services, e.g., Finance | or | Curricular Activity |

[18]

This pattern of administrative organization, with some variations, continues in operation in most school systems throughout the country.[19] The assumption can then be made that (1) this type of organization was copied by educational systems from other enterprises such as the army or industry without regard for its appropriateness; (2) it was copied because it is effective; or (3) it was fortuitously hit upon in response to organizational demands. The second and third assumptions are consistent with our theory. The fact that practically all organizations, with the possible exception of a Friends' meeting, rely on such structure for co-ordination is impressive, but not conclusive, evidence that it is essential to effective co-ordination. However, the imitative impulse is strong, the power to direct intoxicating and difficult to relinquish, and organizational inertia extremely stubborn. Any one of these may account for the persistence of line and staff in education. But, if we can show that, wherever there have been serious and sincere attempts to abandon line co-ordination, it has stubbornly resisted and reappeared, sometimes in disguise, it will strengthen our theory tremendously.

[18] American Association of School Administrators, Eighth Yearbook, *The Superintendent Surveys Supervision* (Washington, D.C., 1930), p. 55.
[19] Skogsberg, *Administrative Operational Patterns*, pp. 47–49.

Imbued with a laudable desire to abolish the implied and overt authoritarianism in line co-ordination, many theorists of educational administration have drawn ingenious designs for organizational structure that eliminate the hierarchical arrangement of the line.[20] Also, many students of the subject think they detect a trend away from this traditional, and almost universal, administrative structure. Spears discovered that nearly all, if not all, the forty school systems he investigated were operating under line and staff, but that many of them were attempting to modify or abandon it. Below are some of the changes that he considered evidence that it was being abandoned:

1. Regular meetings of directors, supervisors, principals, and teachers to discuss policy.

2. Changing the title of director of elementary education to co-ordinator, and the title of supervisor to consultant.

3. The creation of a council of teachers and administrators to establish instructional policy.

4. Scheduling supervisors' visits to high schools so that the principal and the supervisor may have time to visit together.[21]

It is difficult to see how any of these suggested and alleged reforms affects the line-and-staff principle. The regular meetings and councils called to discuss and determine policy are still subject to the line co-ordinating principle as far as organization is concerned. Moreover, there is no definition of policy here; perhaps it refers to instructional procedures, which when decided upon are then subject to co-ordination. Changing the title of director to co-ordinator only bears out our theory that direction of a diversity of activities in their reciprocal relations is a phase of co-ordination. A supervisor may well be, and perhaps should be, a consultant without administrative authority; and this in no way affects the administrative function. And the supervisor may be directed by the principal while he is visiting in the latter's office as well as,

---

[20] See, for example, Skogsberg, *ibid.*, p. 39.
[21] Harold Spears, "Can the Line-and-Staff Principle Unify Instructional Leadership," *Educational Method*, xx (April, 1941), 343-49.

and more subtly than, by written directives. This study, as do so many others,[22] fails to distinguish between the line and staff as an administrative principle for the co-ordination of diverse activities within the educational organization and such matters as policy determination and instructional supervision.

The hypothesis advanced here is that, however ingeniously disguised, the line and staff principle continues to operate in the administration of all organizations. Notwithstanding all the hue and cry against centralization of decision-making in industry as well as in education, it appears to be extremely doubtful that much delegation has been accomplished,[23] and even if there is delegation, it probably is down the line. Wherever we find the co-ordinating phase of the administrative process at work, we shall doubtless find that it depends upon a hierarchical structure. A recent survey of research in this field tends to confirm this opinion:

> In spite of the talk and writing about decentralizing the decision making process, it is clear that the practice is not as widespread as the talk, either in industry or education. Whether the gap between theory and practice is a natural lag in the application of theory, or whether it represents a lack of proof of soundness of theory, is now a question.[24]

If the hypothesis that the co-ordinating function can be performed only by line authority flowing downward through hier-

[22] See William H. Burton and Leo J. Bruackner, *Supervision—A Social Process* (New York: Appleton-Century-Crofts, 1955), Chap. v; Alfred J. Simpson, "A Critique of the Administrative Structure from the Standpoint of Democratic Concepts," *Progressive Education*, xxx (November, 1952), 32–37; Edward J. Sparling, "Evaluating Some Efforts to Achieve Democracy in Administration," *Democracy in the Administration of Higher Education*, Harold Benjamin, ed. (New York: Harper & Brothers, 1950), and Joseph M. Trickett, A *Synthesis of the Philosophies and Concepts of Staff in the Organization of Business, Government, and Education*, doctor's thesis, Stanford University, California, 1953; Abstract: *Dissertation Abstracts*, xiii, 709–10, No. 5, 1953.
[23] See Perrin Stryker, "The Subtleties of Delegation," *Fortune*, li (March, 1955), 94–97.
[24] Roy M. Hall, Frank P. Leathers, and Charles T. Roberts, "Organization of Schools and Administrative Units," *Review of Educational Research*, xxv (October, 1955), 343.

archical ranks is true, it must be viewed as a necessity imposed by the nature of organizations. It is perfectly clear that some organizations are designed deliberately in this fashion. The oldest of them all, the Catholic Church, which has shown no uneasiness at the presence of hierarchies, is definitely organized in this way. The policy-making procedures of the Catholic Church are, to be sure, different from the one we have discussed earlier, but in the matter of co-ordination the Church has an admirable record.[25]

Pittenger has stated that the centralization of decision-making and the line-and-staff principle in educational organizations may be the result of the fact that education is a state function and derives its authority from the law.[26] However, it is not logical to assume that a democratic state and a highly individualistic society would prefer a hierarchical organization for education unless it proved necessary. The argument here is that the hierarchical line has been adopted widely because the nature of organization demands it.

Let us examine briefly a school in operation and note the demands made upon the administration. We shall observe a hypothetical afternoon session of a public high school, which, we trust, is reasonably similar to an actual situation. The regular work of the school is proceeding according to schedule. Teachers, counselors, and students are using the rooms, textbooks, materials, and methods that they have selected and been assigned. The classes have been scheduled so that students could enroll in courses they need and desire; and each student and teacher has an opportunity to eat his lunch in the cafeteria that will not accommodate all of them at the same time. Minor conflicts occur, but on the whole, the administration of the school at the beginning of this after-

[25] "The Roman Catholic Church," *Management Audit, Special Audit,* No. 137 (American Institute of Management, Vol. v, No. 15, February, 1956). For a criticism, see Peter F. Drucker's "The Management Audit of the Catholic Church," *America,* xciv (February 25, 1956), 582–84.
[26] Pittenger, "Principles Underlying the Centralized Plan of School Administrative Organization," *The American School Board Journal,* cxvi (April, 1948), 19.

Co-ordination

noon session is largely routine because co-ordination has been achieved through prior staffing and allocating.

This routine, however, is always subject to minor conflicts, and not infrequently to unusual and unplanned events. On the day that we are observing this hypothetical school, a county-wide science exhibit is being held in the gymnasium-auditorium—it was scheduled at the beginning of the year for another school, but the gymnasium in which it was to be exhibited was not completed in time. Consequently, the rehearsal for the senior play cannot be held in the gymnasium-auditorium and must be moved to the study hall—the regular detention room—or not be held. The girls' soccer team, accompanied by a teacher chaperon, has to leave the building at two o'clock in order to play another school at four o'clock. Some provision must be made for the classes that teacher conducts and, also, for the students who depend upon that bus for transportation. In the midafternoon an accident occurs in the chemistry laboratory injuring a student. During this same afternoon there is the usual run of disciplinary cases, parents calling for their children, visits from salesmen and from college supervisors of student teachers, breakdowns in equipment, and other normal problems connected with the school organization. It is extremely difficult, if not impossible, to visualize any procedure whereby all these activities, both routine and emergency, can be co-ordinated except through line structure, at the apex of which there is one person who has the authority, the time, and the channels of communication to direct all these activities in their complex reciprocal relations.

At another level of educational administration, that of the superintendent of schools, we find a similar complexity of activity that demands co-ordination. Many of these activities are routine, but some are emergencies. Among them are the assignment of new students moving into the district; requests for transfers from students and teachers; the enforcement of attendance laws; the payment of salaries and bills; calendar changes; the replacement necessitated by unexpected resignations; the dismissal of teachers;

the allocation of limited supplies; the adjudication of conflicts; lunchroom management; the provision of buildings and facilities; the passage of bond issues; and the warding off of threats to the operation of the school organization.

The objection is likely to be encountered that the realities, some of them homely, that we have portrayed represent a narrow, management concept of educational administration and that we have emphasized the trivia of the function. We admit that the co-ordinating function of administration is often concerned about what appear to be trivia; but herein lies a paradox: the trivia of an organization's operation are crucially important to its survival.

2. AUTHORITY

The second condition necessary for the co-ordinating function to operate in an organization is the presence of authority. By authority we mean simply the power and the recognized right of the administrator, enforced by whatever sanctions he may employ, to make decisions necessary for the co-ordination of the activities of persons working within an organization. The authority of the administrator to co-ordinate is similar to the teacher's authority to teach. Because of its abuse and its association with antidemocratic institutions, the term authority has acquired a perjorative connotation, and there is a considerable denial of the principle of authority in liberal and democratic societies. We shall, at the outset, try to dispel two erroneous opinions that pervade the literature of educational administration: that authority is always negative, inhibiting, and destructive of freedom; and that administrative organization in its co-ordinating aspect will in a democratic society somehow be able to avoid the authority principle.

The popular notion that authority always invokes commands, restraints, prohibitions, and penalties—thou shalt's and thou shalt not's—overlooks its positive and permissive aspects. Without denying that, at times, authority presents a forbidding mien, even in the most democratic organizations, it must be admitted that it operates benignly and permissively a great part of the time. The teacher has, under the law, social customs of the community, expert knowledge and acceptance by his pupils, the authority to teach and to provide a classroom environment suitable for learning. Likewise, the administrator has the authority to guide the activities of the personnel within the school organization so that they do not conflict and so that both the organization and the individuals belonging to it may accomplish their goals with a sense of stability and security. "In the deepest sense, authority is not 'flectere' but 'augescere,' not to bend but to further." [27]

That the institutions of a society reflect its central attitudes is a simple axiom that accounts for some, but not all, organizational phenomena. The deduction that administration—particularly educational administration, which is so close to community attitudes and beliefs—will avoid the use of authority because it represents the antithesis of democracy, has been made frequently in recent years. However, it has not been demonstrated that this has happened or that it is possible. According to this theory, organization in a democratic society as well as in any other society requires administrative authority. A democratic society may want to limit this authority to those areas where it is essential and to erect safeguards against its abuse, but it can gain little by attempting to disguise the fact that it may be essential.

Recently there seems to be a tendency to recognize the necessity of the hierarchical principle. Niebuhr has stated forthrightly that

> The necessity of gradation of authority and function in any community or common enterprise must be obvious to even the most casual observer. Every school with more than one room is coordinated under the authority of a "principal"; and every school system with more than one school has a superintendent. Most churches have a hierarchy of superintendents, deacons, or bishops. Communities of common work reveal the same gradation of function and authority. A specialized production opera-

[27] Kenneth D. Benne, *A Conception of Authority* (New York: Bureau of Publications, Teachers College, Columbia University, 1943), p. 221.

tion is governed by a foreman, and the total production is governed and coordinated by a "production manager"; the other specialized functions of sales, promotion, and finance each have their manager, or in this latter day "vice presidents." The whole enterprise is governed by a president or general manager, who is usually under the authority of a board of trustees, representing the owners, in the modern case usually multiple owners. The managerial oligarchy has proved more important than the original theories of ownership anticipated, but that is another story. The political order is integrated by the same sort of hierarchical structure.

Democracy has brought arbitrary power under check and made it responsible, but it has not seriously altered the hierarchical structure of the community.[28]

Not only is authority necessary for the administration of education; it is also legitimate. Its sources, which are legal, social, and personal, provide the positive power and the sanctions that make it effective. The legal sources are constitutions, statutes, by-laws, and court decisions. Duly elected or appointed school officials possess legal authority to perform the duties of their position and, under the law, authority flows downward through the hierarchical ranks. For example, the school superintendent may assign teachers to schools, the principal may assign teachers to rooms, and the teacher may assign pupils to seats. Even if the teacher chooses his school and his room, and the pupil his seat, the authority is present and may be invoked in case of conflict. Otherwise, the school organization would be subject to conflict, disturbances, and interference both from within and from without.

Not all the educational administrator's authority derives directly from the law. In numerous cases the extralegal customs and mores of the community supply the authority to act. It is a somewhat curious fact that American society, avowedly democratic, should hold in such high regard an administrative title and should tolerate such an array of hierarchies. These hierarchies are the result of the great numbers of organizations. More than a century ago De

[28] Reinhold Niebuhr, "Liberty and Equality," *Yale Review*, XLVII (Autumn, 1957), 2–3.

Co-ordination

Tocqueville was impressed with the number of organizations or associations in the United States:

> Americans of all ages, all conditions, all dispositions, constantly form associations. They have not only commercial and manufacturing companies, in which all take part, but associations of a thousand other kinds—religious, moral, serious, futile, general or restricted, enormous or diminutive. The Americans make associations to give entertainment, to found seminaries, to build inns, to construct churches, to diffuse books, to send missionaries to the Antipodes; they found in this manner hospitals, prisons, and schools. If it be proposed to inculcate some truth, or to foster some feeling by the encouragement of a great example, they form a society. Whenever, at the head of some new undertaking, you see the government in France, or a man of rank in England, in the United States, you will be sure to find an association.[29]

Whatever the reason for the great number of organizations, they have succeeded in giving administrative positions and titles a great deal of prestige. Administrative titles throng the educational world: presidents, vice-presidents, deans, assistant deans, chairmen, vice-chairmen, heads, co-ordinators, superintendents, deputy superintendents, assistant superintendents, directors, assistant directors, principals, vice-principals, and assistant principals. Such titles and positions are a mark of preferment and prestige, and the expectations of the whole community are that a person holding one of these titles will be responsible for the co-ordination of the activities within his jurisdiction. This proliferation of administrative positions has spread the ranks of hierarchy among many. Democratic society has attempted to hold them responsible, and each administration is expected to exercise, but not abuse, the authority necessary "to manage" successfully the organization to which he is assigned. Therein lies another source of authority for the superintendent, the principal, and the president.

A third source lies within the administrator. Persons working in

[29] Alexis de Toqueville, *Democracy in America*, Part II, Book 2 (New York: New American Library, 1956), p. 108.

an organization accept the authority of the administrator because it is legal, because it is an accepted part of the culture, and because of certain traits in the administrator himself. These are the traits that are essential to the co-ordinating function. They will be discussed at some length.

Personal Traits

In the study of educational administration today, leadership is a word to conjure with; and, when it is preceded by the adjective "democratic," it becomes an open sesame that provides unfailingly the key to the plaguing problems and perennial mysteries of human relations. But for all the discussion about leadership and the reliance placed on it, the concept is vague and the definitions often ambiguous.[30] If we define leadership as statesmanship, i.e., the ability to bring about a state of affairs that the people will in the end find to be good, but which they do not necessarily currently desire, then according to our definition it is something outside educational administration. To be sure, some school administrators possess and exercise this ability, and we should make it perfectly clear that our theory does not say that an administrator should never presume to act in this capacity. We have stated that when he does he is not acting qua administrator; that most administrators do not possess this ability; that it is not expected of administrators

[30] For some of the current literature on the subject, see the bibliography following Cecil A. Gibb's "Leadership," in *Handbook of Social Psychology*, Gardner Lindzey, ed. (Cambridge, Mass.: Addison-Wesley Press, 1954), Vol. II, Chap. 24, pp. 877–920; *Selected Annotated Bibliography on Leadership and Executive Development* (Maxwell Air Force Base, Alabama: Officer Education Research Laboratory, Air Research and Development Command, 1955); Alonzo G. Grace, *Leadership in American Education* (Chicago: University of Chicago Press, 1950); Helen H. Jennings, *Leadership and Isolation* (2nd ed.; New York: Longmans, Green & Company, 1950); and Andrew W. Halpin, "The Leader Behavior and Leadership Ideology of Educational Administrators and Aircraft Commanders," *Harvard Educational Review*, xxv (Winter, 1955), pp. 18–32.

by the public and the policy-making bodies; and that to introduce this function into our professional requirements for administrators is both unrealistic and responsible for producing unnecessary anxiety in our already overburdened profession.

If we define leadership as the ability to apprehend the changing purposes of an organization, then, according to our definition, it is a part of the administrative process. Likewise, if we define it as the ability to secure public support for an organization and its purposes, it is also an administrative function. More specifically, the term "leadership" has been applied to a specific set of conditions related to the co-ordinating function.

As applied to administration, leadership is a personal quality or set of qualities that are required for the co-ordination of the people working with an organization: "The leader is a person who occupies a position of responsibility in coordinating the activities of the members of the group in their task of attaining a common goal." [31] However, the author of this definition of a leader concludes that

> The findings suggest that leadership is not a matter of passive status, or of the mere possession of some combination of traits. It appears rather to be a working relationship among members of a group in which the leader acquires status through active participation and demonstration of his capacity for carrying cooperative tasks through to completion.[32]

This conclusion appears to be somewhat tautological. In the first place, status in an administrative position may be expected to bestow some capacity for leadership both because of its legitimacy and because of the expectations of the position, although it alone does not suffice, and despite the fact that the members of the organization may be ambivalent in their attitude toward authority. Furthermore, to say that any working relationship in which the "capacity for carrying cooperative tasks through to completion"

---

[31] Ralph M. Stogdill, "Personal Factors Associated with Leadership: A Summary of the Literature," *The Journal of Psychology*, xxv (January, 1918), 65.

[32] *Ibid.*, p. 66.

gives administrators a personal leadership status gives us little insight into what this capacity is. The ability to co-ordinate the activities of people working in groups may await its demonstration before it is recognized, and such demonstration may in turn enhance the ability, both by the acceptance of the leader by the people in the organization, and by the increased confidence it gives the leader; but such a definition avoids recognition of the possibility of personal factors that may be responsible for the initial, and, to some measure at least, the continuing success of the co-ordinator.

Research on leadership began with an attempt to discover a unitary trait that would account for it. None has been found. Then the research concentrated on the discovery of a constellation of traits; but this, too, has not been too fruitful, although positive correlations have been found between such traits as intelligence, self-confidence, dominance, sociability and the selection of persons for positions of leadership.[33] In keeping with the *Zeitgeist*, the latest approach to this problem has been through what is called "interactional theory," in which a number of variables are investigated: personality of the leader; attitudes, needs, and problems of the followers; structure of the group; and the nature of the task to be performed. But as Gibb has realized:

> Leadership cannot be exclusively a function of the situation as it is seen by an independent observer, for individual differences clearly affect the social perception of some individuals by others, and consequently play an important part in giving structure to the situation for those who are a part of it.[34]

Some interesting research on leadership has been done by Halpin. From previous research [35] he selected two factors that

[33] Gibb, "Leadership," in *Handbook of Social Psychology*, Vol. II, Chap. 24, pp. 916–17.
[34] *Ibid.*, p. 886.
[35] Andrew W. Halpin, "The Leader Behavior and Leadership Ideology of Educational Administrators and Aircraft Commanders," *Harvard Educational Review*, xxv (1955) pp. 18–31; "The Leadership Behavior and Combat Performance of Airplane Commanders," *Journal of Abnormal Social Psychology*, XLIX (1954), 19–22, and *Studies in Aircrew Composition III. The*

appear to be related to effective leadership, which he referred to as "Initiating Structure-in-Interaction" and "Consideration"; and he attempted to determine how aircraft commanders and school administrators vary, both as to behavior and ideology, in these two factors. "Consideration" is defined as friendship and warm human relations and "Initiating Structure-in-Interaction" as defining the roles and the relationships of the personnel, the patterns of organization, and the channels of communication. As Halpin had expected, school superintendents displayed more "Consideration" and less "Initiating Structure" than aircraft commanders. The assumptions are made that "Consideration" is related to leadership effectiveness in all groups, both formal and informal, and that "Initiating Structure" is a factor required in leadership effectiveness in formal organizations of all kinds. The "Initiating of Structure" concept is very close, indeed, to our idea of co-ordination. When personnel are assigned, spaces and materials allocated, and a schedule of work arranged in an organization, the administrator must have some prevision of how the various persons and the functions they perform will work together. How this ability can be identified *a priori* is another matter, although it may be possible to do so.

The second trait on which we hazard an opinion as having some relation to administrative effectiveness, and particularly for the co-ordinating phase of administration, we shall call "generalism." A. E. said that the specialist should be "on tap not on top"; and Brooks Adams, to whom we referred in an earlier chapter, equated administration with "generalization." There is an old maxim in administration "*Caveamus expertum*"; and the training of administrators has sometimes taken the form of a very general edu-

---

Combat Leader Behavior of B–29 Aircraft Commanders (Bolling Air Force Base, Washington, D.C.: Human Factors Operations Research Laboratory, September, 1953), AFORL Memo. No. Tn–54–7; J. K. Hemphill, "Patterns of Leadership Behavior Associated with Administration Reputations of the Department of a College," *Journal of Educational Psychology*, XLVI (November, 1955), 385–401; and R. Lickert, *Motivational Dimensions of Administration*, (Chicago: Chicago Public Administration Service, 1954), pp. 89–117.

cation, for example, the education of British colonial officials. The temptation to define this term as an antonym to specialism is strong, but that may be somewhat misleading. A specialist may possess this trait, although it is possible that specialization is inimical to it and that the kind of persons who are comfortable in a narrow specialization tend to lack it. It is the ability to make administrative decisions with a minimum of bias for or against any of the activities or specialities within the organization. Generalism is not to be construed as a lack of zeal; rather it includes equal zeal for all the activities that contribute to the attainment of the organization's purposes.

Generalism, as has been indicated above, is not the mere absence of specialization. It is postulated here as a positive trait, perhaps rare, that contributes to success in co-ordination. Psychological research is, at best, only suggestive. While the trait of "generalism" has not come in for investigation, some work has been done on "set" and the ability to surmount it. Maier has contended that variability may be inhibited by the persistence of a single way of looking at a problem.[36] Guetzkow has found that people who are good at acquiring a set are not always equally good at surmounting it when circumstances require it. Men are probably better than women at surmounting set when it is no longer necessary.[37] Apparently somewhat more remotely related is a study by Holzman and Klein, which tends to support the hypothesis of two principles of organization in cognitive functioning—"leveling" and "sharpening" of differences.[38]

The circumstances of administration that require the trait we have referred to as "generalism" are easily illustrated. A Latin

[36] N. R. F. Maier, "Reasoning in Humans: I. On Direction," *Journal of Comparative Psychology*, x (1930), 115–43, and "An Aspect of Human Reasoning," *British Journal of Psychology*, xxiv (October, 1933), 144–55.

[37] Harold Guetzkow, "An Analysis of the Operation of Set in Problem-Solving Behavior," *Journal of Genetic Psychology*, xlv (October, 1951), 219–44.

[38] P. S. Holzman and G. S. Klein, "Cognitive System Principles of Leveling and Sharpening: Individual Differences in Usual Time-Error Assimilation Effects," *Journal of Psychology*, xxxvii (January, 1954), 105–122.

teacher with a zeal for his subject may become principal of a rural high school in which agriculture is an important study. He need not lose his zeal for Latin, but, as an administrator, he must surmount it and become zealous, also, for agriculture, as well as for the other subjects in the curriculum. Furthermore, he must see both Latin and agriculture in their relation to the purposes of the school. The head of a science department in a small college can afford to and, perhaps, should be biased in favor of science, but in his administrative capacity he cannot make effective administrative decisions with a bias in favor of one science. If he becomes dean, he will need to reduce his bias for science to a minimum and become as objective as possible about its relation to other subjects in the curriculum. If by chance he becomes president of a university, he will need to include in his administrative decisions the importance of an even greater number of specialties. Actually, this is precisely what happens. Often, the teacher of a subject who expresses disdain for some other subject upon assuming an administrative position can view the object of his previous scorn in a different light. It has become one of his concerns along with his original enthusiasm.

Generalism may have two important implications for effectiveness in co-ordination: (1) it may enable the administrator to obtain a better perception of his task and the consequences of his decisions; and (2) it may convey the assurance of fairness to the members of the organization. Fairness is not regarded here as possessing value in its own right as generous behavior. Rather it is postulated as a trait necessary for making effective decisions. There is some evidence against this aspect of our theory. In the Purdue University studies, fairness to subordinates appeared to have little relation to administrative achievement, although it was important in developing staff morale.[39] However, in the long run of accomplishing an organization's objectives, the lack of bias and the appearance of fairness may be effective.

[39] Robert L. Hobson, "Some Psychological Dimensions of Academic Administrators," *Studies in Higher Education* (Purdue University), LXXIII, 3–64;

The third quality or trait that may be associated with leadership, in the sense that the term is used here, as well as in other uses, we shall call "charisma." The word "charisma" was introduced by Max Weber to identify a "natural" leadership quality.[40] The concept, although allegedly used in a completely "value-neutral" way, was surrounded by mystical overtones that have not been dispelled: "The natural leaders in distress have been holders of specific gifts of the body and spirit; and these gifts have been believed to be supernatural, not accessible to everybody."[41] Also, it was conceived by Weber as being antithetical to organization, knowing "only inner determination and inner restraint." In our use of the term, we shall divest it of both its supernatural quality and of its incompatibility with bureaucratic organization. The question may arise: What then is left? Charisma, as we define it, is the ability to get people to identify themselves with an organization and its purposes. In a broader context it means the ability to get people to identify themselves with a cause; but when applied to administration it has a somewhat more limited meaning in that the cause is the organization's purpose, rather than the vision or the purpose of an individual. It need not be awesome, although it can be an antidote for the languid, weary futility of bureaucracy.

Perhaps the quality of charisma depends on the administrator's sincere, disinterested, loyalty to an organization and its purposes; on a sense of mission for carrying them out, a loyalty that is unmistakable, unselfconscious, and contagious. Perhaps the administrator who is primarily loyal to the avowed purposes of the school rather than to the extrinsic rewards of the position will be able to succeed in influencing teachers to identify themselves with the school organization. And, perhaps, also, no amount of cant and incantation will endow him with the quality of charisma, unless the loyalty is genuine. Although we have postulated a personal

---

and Jesse C. Rupe, "Some Psychological Dimensions of Business and Industrial Executives," *ibid.*, pp. 65–95.

[40] H. H. Gerth and C. Wright Mills, *From Max Weber: Essays in Sociology* (New York: Oxford University Press, 1946), pp. 245–52.

[41] *Ibid.*, p. 245.

Co-ordination

trait here that enables an administrator to influence people to identify themselves with an organization, we do not pretend to know how it operates.

However, charisma may well be a two-edged sword. It is reasonable to assume that with persons who accept in some degree the purposes of an organization, with those who are neutral, and with many who are opposed, it can be effective. But with those who have a like allegiance to opposing purposes, and with those whose motives are ulterior, it may create uneasiness and animosity. Its power is feared and its sincerity of purpose disconcerting. To avoid the charge of tender-mindedness, we should hasten to add that our theory here is completely nonvaluational: A disinterested loyalty to an "evil" purpose can be as effective as a similar loyalty to a "good" purpose.

Limitations of Co-ordination

It has been asserted that the co-ordinating aspect of administration demands what may be feared as undemocratic structure and authority. However, it should be recalled that in the modification of an organization's purposes or in the adoption of operational policies and procedures, co-ordination is limited by the extent of the necessities of organization. If a school administrator is attempting to discover whether or not the curriculum should be modified, his co-ordinating function with its attendant powers and structure extends only to the maintenance of the organization and the direction of the activities within the organization toward answering the question.[42] Likewise, if procedures for the school are to be determined by students, teachers, custodians, and parents working on time-consuming committees, the administrator has the

[42] See "Organization Chart of the School Policies Council of Denver Public Schools," in G. Robert Koopman, Alice Miel, and Paul J. Misner, *Democracy in School Administration* (New York: Appleton-Century-Crofts, 1943), p. 49.

same kind of co-ordinating responsibility. But once the procedures are adopted, they must be kept in operation by the authoritative direction of the administrator.

Simon has made a distinction between "procedural" and "substantive" co-ordination that may have some relevance for our theory at this point:

> Coordination may be exercised in both a procedural and a substantive sense. By procedural coordination is meant the specification of the organization itself—that is the generalized description of the behaviors and relationships of the members of the organization. Procedural coordination establishes the lines of authority, and outlines the sphere of activity and authority of each member of the organization.
>
> Substantive coordination is concerned with the *content* of the organization's activities. In an automobile factory, an organization chart is an aspect of procedural coordination, while blueprints for the engine block of the car are an aspect of substantive coordination.[43]

Since Simon appears to identify co-ordination with structure or the results of the co-ordinating activity, we shall substitute the process. If in his "procedural coordination" we add to the "general description" of the "behaviors and relationships" of the members of the organization the act of allocating, arranging, and directing, we apparently have the kind of co-ordination that requires the line-and-staff structure. This activity the superintendent engages in when he assigns teachers to schools. It is more difficult to draw an analogy between his example of substantive co-ordination and the work of the educational administrator. Presumably the blueprint of the engine block would correspond to the objectives of a ninth-grade science course and the means by which these objectives can be obtained, but it is not so easy in the latter example to relate the means to the ends. It is this type of co-ordination that has been partly responsible for the reaction in education to the methods of

---

[43] Herbert A. Simon, *Administrative Behavior* (New York: The Macmillan Company, 1955), pp. 140–41.

business administration. Apparently, there must be substantive co-ordination in education—first-year French, for example, should be taught so that students will be able to begin second-year French—but its applicability for education has serious limitations. The failure to construct an engine block according to the blueprint would prove to be a disaster to industry; but in education the unfortunate results may be quite transient. As a matter of fact, an emphasis on substantive co-ordination might be inimical to the teaching activity. Perhaps it can well be done informally by the teachers themselves.

A final note of clarification should be given, particularly for those readers who are familiar with the classical literature on the subject. Our theory of co-ordination does not make mandatory the exclusive use of any one, or any special combination, of the four theoretical bases for organization: (1) by major purpose; (2) by major process; (3) by clientele; and (4) by place.[44] The school organization exists for the accomplishment of certain purposes, interrelated and arranged in a more or less stable hierarchy of importance; it requires a variety of processes and skills; and it serves a clientele made up largely, but not exclusively, of the younger members of society. In the planning, allocating, and directing of the activities within the school, all of these aspects must be taken into consideration, often at the same time.

[44] Luther H. Gulick, "The Theory of Organization," in *Papers on the Science of Administration*, pp. 21–30.

CHAPTER VI

Public relations

EDUCATIONAL ADMINISTRATION faces in two directions. In the description of the discernment of purpose it is apparent that administration looks outward; in co-ordination its activity is almost entirely within the organization; and in its third major activity, that of obtaining support, it looks outward again. This third function we refer to as public relations.

Justification for public relations in educational administration has rested on both moral and practical considerations. The usual warrants are well known and somewhat trite, but nonetheless valid: (1) the right of the people in a democracy to know what their schools are doing; (2) the obligation on the part of those who run the schools to know what the people want of their schools; and (3) the necessity of securing public support for education. A logical justification can now be added: if administration is given the responsibility for the maintenance and effectiveness of an organization within a society of competing organizations, it follows that the administrator is called upon to inform, solicit, and persuade, by legitimate means, both subtle and direct, in order to obtain outside support. As the number of organizations competing for support increases, and as their legitimate purposes expand, administration's quest for public support becomes more urgent and intense. Before examining in detail the implications of this aspect of our theory, we shall first attempt to define public relations.

Definition

The earlier phrase, "school publicity," reminiscent of press agentry and somewhat incongruous with the mores of the education profession, has given way almost entirely to the more respectable "public relations." The same trend toward professional dignity and reserve has occurred in business and probably politics, in both because the term publicity has acquired an aura of banality. But whatever ambitions are revealed by the substitution, a theoretical distinction between publicity and public relations has been maintained. In "public relations" administration attempts to discover what the public, or, in current language, "the publics," expect of the organization, as well as to create a favorable public attitude toward an organization or its products.

Even the term "public relations" has seemed to be too unacademic. Moehlman coined "social interpretation" as a more appropriate substitute, and he defined it as the

> recognition and satisfaction of institutional responsibility for locating, defining, and crystallizing unexpressed and undefined social feelings, desires, and wills. It seeks clarification and definiteness in expressions of the social will through methods of democratic education which include presentation of all known facts and complete freedom of discussion of these facts by the people.[1]

[1] Arthur B. Moehlman, *Social Interpretation* (New York: D. Appleton-Century Company, 1938), p. 106.

So far this definition corresponds closely to our theory that the discernment of purpose is an administrative function. Moehlman, however, goes on to list the objectives of the interpretative function: (1) to develop continuing public consciousness of the importance of the educational process in a democratic social order; (2) to establish confidence in the functioning institution; (3) to furnish adequate means to maintain its efficient operation; and (4) to enlist parental or community support for specific measures.[2] Now if these are the real objectives of social interpretation as it as defined above, one must assume one of the following: (1) the discovery of the social will is necessary in order to set up the organization's objectives in conformity to it, and such a procedure will obviate the necessity for public relations in the sense of securing public support; (2) the social will, once discerned, shall be directed, unwittingly on its part, toward accepting and supporting the organization's objectives; or (3) the author failed to see the inconsistency between his definition of social interpretation and its objectives as he listed them. It is possible, of course, that he assumes that the objectives education professors hold for education are synonymous with those implicit in the social will.

A similar trend away from the conception of public relations as an activity designed exclusively to create favorable attitudes toward, and to secure public support for, an organization appears in much of the writing on the subject outside of education. Public relations has three meanings, according to Bernays: (1) information given to the public; (2) persuasion directed at the public to modify attitudes and actions; and (3) efforts to integrate attitudes and actions of an institution with its publics and of publics with that institution.[3] The task of integrating the attitudes and actions of an institution or organization with its public means, first of all, that the administration must know what the public expects of the organization and must adjust its activities accordingly. Second, it

---

[2] *Ibid.*, pp. 106–107.
[3] Edward L. Bernays, *Public Relations* (Norman: University of Oklahoma Press, 1952), p. 3.

means that the public must understand the objectives and the problems of the organization. And, finally, such integration apparently avoids dealing with the problem of interorganizational relations.

In a later book, somewhat disturbingly entitled *The Engineering of Consent*,[4] Bernays gives a forthright definition: "Public relations is the attempt, by information, persuasion, and adjustment, to engineer public support for an activity, cause, movement, or institution." This simple, straightforward definition of the essential nature of the public relations activity is refreshing in the stifling atmosphere of circumlocution and periphrase, e.g., the prevalence of such euphemisms as "social interpretation," "advertorials," and "information services." Organizations may not be competing with one another in their objectives, but they are doing so in their efforts to secure public support. For instance, the state department of highways and the state department of education have separate, worthy, and desirable over-all objectives, the achievement of which is, in the main, sanctioned by the public will. To a considerable degree, the administrator of each organization will be faced with the responsibility of obtaining the initial or continuing support necessary for the organization to accomplish these objectives. The public relations function, therefore, is simply the effort to secure support for the activities that are essential to carry out the accepted purposes.

The most cursory observation will reveal that a considerable portion of the work that is labeled administrative is spent in securing financial and moral support for an organization. Although the "publics" may differ somewhat for public and private educational organizations, and the sources of financial support vary from the custodians of public funds to the possessors of private wealth, the function of public relations remains fundamentally the same. Politics, persuasion, and publicity are employed by administration in order to gain support for the organization.

Our definition is as follows: Public relations is that activity

[4] Norman: University of Oklahoma Press, 1955. P. 4.

which is deliberately pursued for the sake of obtaining support for an organization in order that it may survive and accomplish its purposes. In the case of public education these objectives are those that have been accepted by the public will and are expressed through constitutional provisions, laws, by-laws, and the rulings of boards of education; and it is in the obtaining of support for these objectives only that public relations, as we have defined the term, has a place in educational administration.

Now it is true, as we have pointed out in an earlier chapter, that the public will for educational objectives is not unanimous. There will always be people who are unconcerned about or opposed to at least some of the objectives and purposes of the schools. These differences the administrator must carry in the margin of his ledger on the public will, but at the same time he has to present to all groups as favorably as possible the school's accepted purposes. Certainly, he has the obligation to support these purposes, to apprise the community of the cost of accomplishing them, and to solicit support. However subtle his presentation and however devious the route from public relations to public contribution, the end is always the same: to gain support for the organization. Whether it is a blatant and urgent appeal for funds or a subtle and artistic poster, play, or pageant; whether it is a school principal in a crossroads town soliciting the local Parent Teacher Association for funds to purchase a projector, or the president of an Ivy League university adroitly cultivating wealthy alumni, the function is essentially the same. If there is some element of public accounting, some reporting on stewardship, in this kind of activity, it is usually designed to avert criticism and to insure a continuing favorable attitude toward the organization.

The public relations function can be distinguished from the other administrative functions. In large organizations the administrative offices may include a public relations division. The members of this division have the primary responsibility of carrying out this function of administration. However, the director of public relations may have also a co-ordinating responsibility for the direction of the activities of his staff. Likewise, the chief administrator has the responsibility for co-ordinating this branch of his administrative personnel. But if he or his subordinates meet with public groups, send out greeting cards, make public speeches, or appear in any way as a representative or symbol of the organization, he is performing public relations. If teachers are expected to assume some chore of the responsibility for securing public support for education, it may be recognized that they are performing administrative duties.

The Legitimacy of Public Relations

The relation between legitimacy and necessity need not be fully explored for us to realize that if the public relations function is essential to administration, its legitimacy is likely to be inferred. However, it is difficult to find in the literature on the subject a clear and unequivocal statement that public relations, in the sense of soliciting public support, is a legitimate function of administration. Particularly is this true in the literature on educational and public administration.[5] The political prestige and power of the administrator in modern government has made the legislative bodies uneasy about any activity that might enhance his influence. Also, in educational organizations, the general distaste of the scholar, the teacher, or the academician for anything that is redolent of salesmanship has brought disparagement of public relations, although they expect the organization to be supported. Part of their attitude also may be due not only to what they consider the banalities of advertising but also to their fear of administrative power and prestige: "Dr. D. W. Logan, the Principal of London University, takes my name in vain in his Annual Report. He is one of those administrators who today have all

[5] Herbert A. Simon, Donald W. Smithburg, and Victor A. Thompson, *Public Administration* (New York: Alfred A. Knopf, 1950), pp. 415–22.

the honour and power."[6] If it is necessary for the educational administrator to pursue such an activity, a clear statement of this necessity should be made. That it is necessary we shall now attempt to demonstrate.

The maxim "Who wills the ends, wills the means" cannot be construed to mean that once the ends of an organization are clearly agreed upon, the means will be automatically forthcoming. The will for the ends apparently is not enough to provide the means. Organizations, for all their numbers, lead a precarious existence; the Roman Catholic Church and a few universities are the only organizations that can claim a long, continuous history: "Failure to cooperate, failure of cooperation, failure of organization, disorganization, disintegration, destruction of organization —and reorganization—are characteristic facts of human history."[7]

This ephemeral nature of organizations may be explained by a variety of causes. First, it should be noted that most organizations are not formed for the accomplishment of perpetual purposes, and once their purposes are accomplished, they should, and frequently do, disintegrate, although their existence is often prolonged beyond the time of their usefulness. Second, the survival of an organization depends upon the maintenance of an internal equilibrium, which can be achieved only by effective co-ordination. Third, "the preponderance of persons in a modern society always lies on the negative side with reference to any particular existing or potential organization . . . most of the persons existing in society are either indifferent to or positively opposed to any single one of them."[8] And, fourth, our theory holds that even when an organization has a continuing purpose, such as an educational organization, when it has effective co-ordination, and when the preponderance of public opinion lies on the positive side, as it does for most of the purposes of education, the survival of the organiza-

[6] John Betjeman, "City and Suburban," *Spectator*, cxcvi (June 8, 1956), 788.
[7] Chester I. Barnard, *The Functions of the Executive* (Cambridge, Mass.: Harvard University Press, 1954), p. 5.
[8] *Ibid.*, p. 84.

tion often depends upon the efforts of the administration to obtain material and psychological support.

As has been indicated, the practical concern for the legitimacy of public relations in tax-supported organizations arises from the fear that public money will be used for public relations or propaganda to change, perpetuate, or expand the original purposes. Since the same mechanisms may be used to change and expand purposes as are used to obtain support for existing and accepted purposes, the over-all policy-making agencies have been reluctant to endow the administrator with the means that might be used to obtain support for the achievement of the accepted purposes. This situation seems to prevail in government, in public education, and in other organizations in which the purposes are likely to be somewhat ambiguous or intangible, and where they are undergoing change. Such skepticism is probably well founded. Clark found that an organization whose purposes were not well established tended to transform them by adjusting them to take care of what appeared to be emerging needs in society.[9]

The bounds of this skepticism may be illustrated by the range of opportunities for the educational administrator. At one extreme we may find that the purposes of education are clearly understood and relatively static, the cost carefully calculated, and the budget approved. When these conditions obtain, the "legitimate" public relations function of the administrator would consist only of such activities as announcing the calendar, reporting the progress of the students, and representing the educational organization at public events. It is true that he will be concerned with keeping the level of support where it is and also looking for continuing support, but, in this hypothetical situation, his public relations responsibility is extremely limited. At the other extreme, we can imagine a situation in which the purposes of the educational organization are enormously confused, vague, and changing, and in which the administrator is compelled to solicit support with

[9] Burton R. Clark, "Organizational Adaptation and Precarious Values: A Case Study," *American Sociological Review*, xxi, No. 3 (June, 1956), 327–36.

energy and force in order to maintain the schools. His public relations function in this instance is likely to become confused with his responsibility for the discernment of purpose; but although the latter is logically prior to the former, he will find himself in the position of soliciting support for the organization as it is and at the same time providing the mechanisms whereby the purposes may be clarified. If this distinction is borne in mind, the legitimacy of public relations would not be subject to such suspicious scrutiny.

In practical situations, however, the bounds of public relations are not so clear. The difficulty of expressing clearly and concretely the purposes of an educational organization, the lack of agreement in the amount of support needed, and the peril to over-all policy-making agencies of placing highly effective publicity techniques in the hands of energetic administrators, all serve to cast suspicion upon the practice of appropriating public means for public relations. Scarcely a public school system has a public relations office under that name. Also in the federal government the Congress in 1913 prohibited by act the payment of money to any employee called a "publicity expert," unless specific appropriations authorized such payments.[10]

Again, in 1930, in order to thwart some of the New Deal administrative agencies, the Congress prohibited federal agencies from sending informational materials through the mail free of charge unless they were requested to do so.[11] The reason for this restriction is obviously the distrust on the part of Congress of the administrative agencies, the fear that the latter will use public funds to expand their role or to extend the duration of their agencies beyond that intended by the legislature. Now, since the agency must perform a public relations function if it is to accomplish its purposes, if not to secure funds, then, at heart, to create good will and obtain moral support, the position of "information officer" has often been established. The Federal Bureau

[10] 38 Stat. L. 212.
[11] Simon, Smithburg, and Thompson, *Public Administration*, p. 417.

Public Relations

of Investigation, for example, would find it difficult to carry out its duties, if it did not enjoy a favorable attitude on the part of the public.

School administration is different only in respect to the fact that the over-all policy-making powers reside in boards of education as well as in state legislatures and in the fact that the administrator must work more directly with the problem of raising funds to carry out the policies for education. The crucial question that the administrator should ask himself and all public organizations is whether his public relations effort is being used to secure support for accepted purposes or for changes in purpose. If he is sure that it is for the former, he can legitimately be vigorous and importunate in his publicity. For to him is given the responsibility of maintaining an organization and of carrying out certain educational programs. Not to solicit support, when needed, would be but to neglect his responsibility. But, on the other hand, if the purposes are unclear, according to our theory of administration, he is obligated to attempt to clarify them, while at the same time attempting to engage public support for the purposes agreed upon, and for whatever activity is necessary for the further clarification of purposes.

This definition of public relations can and does include those "informing" activities that are essential to the creation of public understanding. In the educational organization, these fall into two categories: (1) those related to organizational matters, e.g., announcing dates for holidays; and (2) those related directly to the intrinsic purposes of the school, e.g., explaining to parents why a certain method of teaching reading has been adopted. Both types of public information can be warranted by the logical necessities of our theory of administration, and it is not necessary to invoke the principle of rights of the constituents to know what its public organizations are up to, however valid such a justification may be. The announcement of the calendar contributes directly to the functioning of the organization, and it may also contribute to the development of favorable attitudes. The same thing may be said for the information on teaching methods. Both are, therefore, legitimate public relations procedures.

A common stereotype of the kind of information about their organizations that administrators are likely to give is "Everything is always all right according to the front office." Administrators do show an uneasiness about the kind of information that is given out. This attitude may be attributed to the fact that they want it to be as accurate as possible, but it is probably true that they often color it in favor of the organization. If this is true, two reasons are apparent. The first is personal; an administrator naturally would like to create a favorable impression about his own ability. To indicate that there are serious problems, partial successes, and even outright failures may throw some doubt on his ability to direct the organization. It is likely that administrators generally are oversensitive about the public expectations, but it is understandable why they do not prefer to air all the realities of their difficult and complex responsibilities.

The second reason arises from the nature of organizational life. The "judicious" Hooker once said:

> He that goeth about to persuade a multitude, that they are not so well governed as they ought to be, shall never want attentive and favourable hearers; because they know the manifold defects whereunto every kind of regiment is subject, but the secret lets and difficulties, which in public proceedings are innumerable and inevitable, they have not ordinarily the judgment to consider.[12]

From the enemies of the organization, as well as from his own personal enemies, the administrator tends to keep any information that can be used against either. In educational organizations the vagueness and the remoteness of the goals, and, particularly, the difficulty in obtaining concrete evaluations enlarge the opportunity

[12] Richard Hooker, *The Laws of Ecclesiastical Polity* (London: Everyman's Library, 1954), Vol. I, Book I, p. 148.

for criticism. It is impossible to prepare an accurate statement of profit and loss.

The logical basis of the public relations function is implicit in our definition of administration. That this aspect of the administrative activity has been abused has no doubt been due in part to an unclear notion of the administrative responsibility. If public relations is recognized as the responsibility for obtaining support for accepted purposes, the uneasiness of the over-all policy-making agencies should disappear. Also, the public administrator, including the superintendent of schools, would need feel no doubt about the propriety of his actions while he is engaged in the competitive solicitation for public support. Part of the ambivalence toward such solicitation, the tendency to disguise its real nature by couching it in euphemistic phrases, and the suspicion that it has engendered may be due to the fact that it is an activity that may be used for propaganda and for the changing of organizational purposes.

Public Relations and Social Planning

The attempt to define and to justify the public relations aspect of educational administration has doubtless left the impression that the interorganizational world is competitive—a social jungle in an era when co-operation and planning are recommended. This is the impression we expect to make, for, in both planned and unplanned society, organizations must compete somewhere along the line for public support.

Looking at education only in our unplanned society, we find that independent schools compete with public schools and with other independent schools for students, finances, and public good will. These organizations have individual histories. They have grown up independently of each other, the result of habits, unconscious desires, deliberate purposes, and compromises. Each organization is struggling to exist. Public educational organizations compete directly with other governmental organizations for fiscal support, not only through official channels but also by direct appeals to the taxpayers for approval of tax levies. The quest for funds is complicated by the fact that three tiers of government are involved—local, state, and national—and also by the fact that in many instances the school officials must go directly to the people; in Ohio, for example, because of the ten-mill tax limitation, school boards and superintendents must engage in publicity campaigns periodically to get the people to vote for local revenue measures in order to participate in state funds. At the same time that state school superintendents are seeking financial support from legislatures, and city superintendents are trying to influence aldermen, councilmen, and budget directors, the administrators of independent and parochial schools, which also perform an educational function, may be soliciting financial support from the individuals and corporations in the community that are most affected by the tax measures for public education.

As we view the kind of organizational competition that prevails, we are compelled to ask: Can we expect anything other than guerrilla warfare among organizations, and will not the most predatory gain the largest share of the taxpayer's dollar, the philanthropist's trust, the widow's mite? Can we expect anything other than competitive strife between public education and public highways, for example? Between public and private universities? Between public and private schools? Many sociologists and political scientists deplore this situation, not because they find the competition uncongenial, but because they see in this system gross inefficiency and waste:

> Let us take another example, a community of ten thousand people. A study will reveal that there are eighty-five to a hundred organized groups and formally established agencies operating in the community. We find among these agencies and organized groups twenty which are particularly concerned with

children and youth, and we may find them getting into each other's hair a bit: some bickering and jealousies, a lot of misunderstanding as to what each is doing. The need, of course, is for some type of coordination and planning.[13]

This same sociologist goes on to describe, by way of contrast, the River Rouge plant in Detroit, which is organized into many departments, and the proper relationships between these departments in operation is stressed as vital to successful organization. He does admit that the careful planning and co-ordination that are responsible for the smooth-running efficiency and lack of conflict are largely dictatorial. Communities, on the other hand, remain competitive, democratic in that they lack direction from a supreme administrative agency, unco-ordinated, and inefficient. According to his estimate they operate at somewhere between twenty and fifty per cent of the efficiency of River Rouge.

A pleasant and recurring dream of many political scientists has as its main theme the integration of school administration with local government. This dream may arise from the *id* of a special discipline, but it is consciously justified by the insistence that such integration would eliminate duplication and waste. Realizing that dreams are realizable only in part, the political scientist is ordinarily willing to settle for voluntary co-operation between schools and other public agencies. Of legitimate concern to any student of government is the hodgepodge of governmental units "often specialized and unifunctional, possessing unique boundaries and resembling each other only in ability to tax, stacked on one another like a child's blocks in impossible appearing stages of imbalance." [14]

The implications of the suggestion for more co-ordination of the inter-organizational activity of the modern community will be examined later when the social role of educational adminis-

[13] Gordon W. Blackwell, "A Sociologist on School Community Relations," *The Annals of the American Academy of Political and Social Science*, cccii (November, 1955), 128–35.
[14] Eldon G. Johnson, "Coordination: the Viewpoint of a Political Scientist," *ibid.*, pp. 136–42.

tration is discussed. Here we are primarily concerned with public relations. This question, therefore, seems appropriate: What is the function of the public relations activity in a society that appears to be moving in the direction of more voluntary co-operation and planning?

The assumption has been made that, because organizations compete for public support, administration, through its public relations activity, must engage in this competition. Also, it is apparently true that in order for some organizations to accomplish their objectives, they must have the understanding and the good will of the public. Obviously then, in a co-ordinated community, this second need for public relations would be essential. But what would happen to the competitive solicitation for support, if an allocation of public functions and resources were made by some supreme co-ordinating agency? To answer this question, we shall look at a community where this has been done.

Liverpool, England, offers an example of community co-ordination. Here one finds a County Borough Council that functions through standing committees. The presence of councillors on more than one committee enables them to view the various public agencies in relation to one another. Within the County Borough Council there is a Finance and General Purpose Committee, whose duty it is to assess the relative priorities of the programs "which must compete to some extent with each other, unless no limit is set on the call rate. . . ."[15] And, significantly for us, "as education is now by far the largest spending service left to local government, the Education Committees of County and Borough Councils are particularly apt to be involved in such tensions." Apparently, it is expected that the Education Committee will compete with other powerful committees, such as the housing committee. This competition occurs within the co-ordinating council, rather than, as in an unco-ordinated American community, outside the governmental agencies. To what extent the

[15] H. S. Magnay, "Liverpool: A Case Study in Coordination," *ibid.*, pp. 88–99.

Public Relations

Education Committee attempts to bring public pressure to bear on the Council cannot be determined from this description, but insofar as it does, its public relations function is not fundamentally unlike that in an unco-ordinated community. In any event education is in competition with other public agencies at the Council level.

Practice and Propriety

Having demonstrated both the necessity for the public relations function and its logical connection with administration, we shall now discuss some general matters of procedure. First we shall place the responsibility for the performance of public relations, and then we shall attempt to arrive at some tentative guides to practice based on the criteria of effectiveness and appropriateness.

The conclusion that follows immediately upon the previous section is that, if public relations is an aspect of administration, we should expect that it is to be done by administrative personnel. Although the separation of functions in an organization can never be so clear cut as they are in an armchair analysis, this expectation is reasonably practical. This is not to say that the teacher has no public relations responsibility in the school—certainly the teacher-child and the teacher-parent relationship is fraught with public relations possibilities—but in teaching, counseling, research, and any other intrinsic activity, it would probably be harmful to this activity in the long run for the teacher to be concerned continually with whether or not his teaching would attract or repel public support for the organization. Furthermore, the qualities necessary for good teaching may not be those required for effective public relations. Public speaking, lobbying, advertising, and the many varieties of Dale Carnegie-ism may not be the teacher's forte, nor should he be judged on the basis of these talents. On the other hand, an administrator is expected to be somewhat proficient in this respect. His day-by-day activities demand that he meet the public in a variety of situations and that he create a favorable attitude toward the schools. A superintendent or principal who spends two hours each week at a service club luncheon is on duty; the hours he spends in such activity are working time.

Lack of recognition of the nature of and the necessity for public relations can be a source of conflict between administrators and academic personnel. First, there is a kind of traditional disdain among intellectuals for the salesmanship involved. The level of public relations cannot rise far above or fall far below the understanding and tastes of the groups that it is designed to influence; and, while there may be some tendency to underestimate this level, there will likely be some discrepancy between the ideals of the academicians in these matters and the practical requirements. Particularly is this likely to be true in public organizations. Second, the administrator, who must engage in these affairs, may be impatient with the academician, who finds the world outside the grove a vulgar place, who does not want to be a "regular fellow," and who consistently engages in understatement. And, third, there is always the possibility that the teacher who works obscurely in the classroom will resent the administrator's opportunity for public contacts, prominence, and publicity. Recognition that public relations is a necessary weapon for the organization's survival should enhance its status as an administrative responsibility. The critical instinct that is important in the classroom is of limited value in the competition of obtaining public support.

Principles of public relations in educational organizations are numerous and fairly uniform. Based on what are considered criteria of effectiveness and appropriateness, they include maxims such as: (1) public relations should be continuous; (2) public relations should be honest; and (3) public relations should be based on the intrinsic work of the school.[16] Reasonable as these

[16] See American Association of School Administration, Twenty-eighth Yearbook, *Public Relations for America's Schools* (Washington, D.C., 1950).

principles appear to be, there is a great scarcity of facts about their effectiveness. Like principles of advertising in general, they are difficult to evaluate in terms of results. Some studies have been made of specific techniques,[17] but on the whole the principles are based on impressions and moral and aesthetic considerations. It is on these more general considerations that we are forced to rely in setting up general guide lines for public relations practice.

Since educational organizations are concerned with accomplishing goals that are remote, somewhat intangible, and usually not urgent, the activity designed to secure public support may well have to be vigorous and continuous. Education is not an easy commodity to sell. One of its numerous paradoxes is that, although it is held in high esteem, it is often inadequately supported. To be sure, its more tangible and practical aspects are comparatively readily supported; for example, funds are forthcoming for aspects of education that are related to national defense. But those aspects that accomplish the more remote and intangible objectives of the schools usually require vigorous activity in order to gain support. Noble, humanitarian, aesthetic, and purely intellectual purposes, although accepted by the public, usually are not accomplished without strenuous effort. It follows, then, that the public relations activity must be exercised in behalf of the objectives that are difficult to support even more than it is exercised for those for which support is relatively easy to obtain. And because of the nature of things, the school's external relations must adjust to the harsh exigencies of the world outside. The temptation is great for the administrator to concentrate on these aspects of education that are easily supportable, for in so doing he can record success. It is clearly logical that public relations for education must accept the responsibility of supporting all its accepted purposes and the means thereto, however difficult the task may be.

The second principle is that the content of the publicity for education should be the intrinsic purposes and activities of the educational organization. Here we have some empirical evidence

[17] See, for example, John Allen Smith's *An Appraisal of School Board Techniques* (Los Angeles: University of Southern California Press, 1934).

for our recommendation.[18] Although learning, research, rehearsals, and teaching are often pedantic, slovenly, unpredictable, and inefficient affairs and do not fit the stereotypes of good public relations exhibits, they are interesting and appropriate. We know that pupil progress, methods of teaching, teachers, discipline, and character training all rank high in the priorities for publicity. Not only do they represent the accepted work of the school, but they are the aspects of education in which most people are interested. Nor are they incompatible with modern publicity techniques; a rehearsal can be televised as easily as the final concert, and the procedures by which a child is taught to read are as easily portrayed as the child reading a well-rehearsed piece.

When it comes to the matter of taste, propriety, and appropriateness in public relations, the administrator faces the dilemma of professionalism and advertising. Certainly he will be concerned about integrity, honesty, and good taste, but he will also be concerned about effectiveness. Impaled on the horns of this dilemma, he often achieves neither. The final principle of public relations that is recommended here is that if the content of the publicity for education is honest and intrinsic, the method may be modern, vigorous, and even blatant. Or if subtle, suggestive publicity is more effective, it can be used with great ingenuity also. The only other safeguard is one that has been mentioned before: The administrator should be sure that he is seeking support for an accepted purpose. Otherwise, he will not be effective.

[18] See, for example, Belmont Farley, *What to Tell the People about the Public Schools* (New York: Teachers College, Columbia University, 1929) and *The Public Looks at Education*, Report No. 21 (Denver: National Opinion Research Center, August, 1944).

Before we attempt to speculate on the relations between the two, it is necessary that we inquire into the nature of education.

Varieties of Education

The nature of education is a subject of continuing and widespread controversy. At first glance it may appear somewhat surprising that so little is definitely known about the nature of an activity so ancient and universal, but this very universality, as well as the inherent mysteries of learning, may be partly responsible for our ignorance. Education is so commonplace a thing that, although in rare and deliberate moments we may marvel at its phenomena, normally they do not awe or intrigue us. Perhaps more surprising is the reluctance to accept what is fairly well established as scientific knowledge about education, and the apparent desire to keep education as a subject for mere opinion. However, even at the most casual level of observation, there are some characteristics that are immediately striking and incontrovertible. One of these is the variety of organizations devoted to the enterprise. With this characteristic, we shall begin our inquiry into the nature of education.

The forms, levels, and types of education are extremely diverse. Groton, the Colorado School of Mines, St. Johns on the Severn, the public high school in Abilene, the kindergarten at the Cathedral Church of the Incarnation, the Huntington Township Consolidated School, the Naval Academy, Arthur Murray's, and the International Correspondence Schools are all educational institutions. The genera of schools include nursery schools, junior colleges, land grant colleges, conservatories, and finishing schools. Whatever education is or does, it is organized in a great variety of institutions.

A closer look reveals that this pluralism in education is not confined to its external forms; it is continued within the organizations. Philosophies, objectives, curriculums, and procedures are even more diverse than the institutions themselves. Widely ranging traditional philosophers of education continue to have their disciples; Plato, St. Ignatius, Dewey, and a throng of lesser pedagogical theorists contend for acceptance. And within the traditional theories the variations are innumerable. As a matter of fact, so numerous, overlapping, and ambiguous are the theories of what education is, or what it should be, that it is possible to give them only very general classification. Education is regarded as growth, the preparation for democratic living, the training of the intellect, creative expression, habit formation, the acquisition of the cultural heritage, problem-solving, vocational preparation, biological and social adjustment, character development, the cultivation of discriminating tastes, or any combination of these, and many additional theories. Dewey, for example, whose name is associated inseparably with the idea of education as growth, also viewed it as the transmission of the cultural heritage.[2] The philosophies of education vary and imbricate.

Dissimilarities characterize curriculum and method also; they become the subjects of vigorous, and sometimes dogmatic, proposals and counterproposals. The current public interest in education has brought its diversity into public view, but, doubtless, the histories of education that deal with its essentials are forced to portray a continuous stream of suggestions and renewed suggestions about what education is and what it should do. The persistence of many notions about curriculum and method is no less astounding than their variety. Thomas Huxley used the Thames basin as a unifying factor in his "core curriculum" for children at the Royal Institution in 1869;[3] and Harold Alberty of Ohio State University is also an exponent of the "core cur-

[2] See John Dewey, *Democracy and Education* (New York: The Macmillan Company, 1928), Chap. 1.
[3] Thomas Huxley, *Physiography* (New York: D. Appleton and Company, 1882), Chap. 1.

riculum," but he would substitute adolescent "needs and interests" as the unifying factor.[4]

This variety in the outward appearances can be solely a reflection of the fact that very little is known about education; hence the occasion for so many divergent forms and dogmatic theories. If this is true, the variety is good, since on the basis of scant knowledge it would be unwise to entrust education to one method, one curriculum, or one theory. Another hypothesis, and one equally plausible, although it may run counter to the tendency to simplicity, is that education is by its very nature an extremely complex activity that demands a pluralism of institutions and purposes, of curriculums and methods. Therefore, to force an elegant simplicity of forms and functions on an enormously complicated activity might well be inimical to the enterprise. Plausible also is the hypothesis that the variety in education stems in part from the intensely personal and egotistic [5] nature of teaching. Most teachers probably believe, and for effectiveness should believe, that their method, their subject, their manner are indispensable in anything that might reasonably be called education. Charles Lamb observed this trait in schoolmasters:

> One of these professors, upon my complaining that these little sketches of mine were anything but methodical, and that I was unable to make them otherwise, kindly offered to instruct me in the method by which young gentlemen in *his* seminary were taught to compose English themes.[6]

[4] Harold Alberty, *Reorganizing the High-School Curriculum* (New York: The Macmillan Company, 1953).
[5] This term is applied here only to the classroom manner of the teacher. Whether this characteristic extends beyond the classroom is a difficult matter to determine, since teachers apparently exhibit unaggressive behavior with other adults.
[6] "The Old and the New Schoolmaster" in *The Complete Works and Letters of Charles Lamb* (New York: The Modern Library, 1935), p. 49 (italics mine).

The Paradoxes of Education

Somewhat less apparent than its diversity, but equally typical, are the paradoxes of education. Education is at once important and trivial, sublime and ridiculous, honored and rejected, creative and habituating. Therefore, the prevailing attitudes toward it are likely to be ambivalent.

The fact that education is both important and trivial is the source of considerable nonsense and lack of realism. Many of its ends and procedures are inevitably petty, homely, and trifling. To take a somewhat indelicate example from the lower levels of education, that of toilet training, we can readily see how a concern about so commonplace a matter, which Uncle Toby Shandy said should be wiped up and not mentioned further, may have consequences for the classroom and, allegedly, for the development of the child's personality. But whether or not they have more important and remote consequences, matters of this kind are inevitably the business of the lower schools, and the task of teaching is indissolubly connected with them. It is true that some of the more glamorous professions, medicine, for example, concern themselves with activities of the same order, but usually only with their pathology. Teaching, on the contrary, assists the normal, unspectacular maturation of the immature.

Selecting a more academic example, or at least a less vital one, we note the pedantic interests of one of the great pedagogues of literature. An eminent classical and humanities scholar in his commentary on the famous "Carpe diem" ode of Horace takes meticulous pains to point out, not the destiny of man that is expressed in *Tū nē quaesieris, scīre nefās, quem mihi, quem tibi finem dī dederint* . . . , but that *nē* with the perfect subjunctive is a more pre-emptory colloquial prohibition than *nē* with the present subjunctive, or the normal polite periphrasis with *noli*.[7] This sort of emphasis has created the pedagogical manner that dwells in the schools. This insistence upon fine distinctions and obscure technicalities surrounds the educational enterprise with an aura of paltriness and pedantry. The paradox lies in the fact that such petty concerns have a way in the long run and en masse of becoming enormously important:

> Balston, our tutor, was a good scholar after the fashion of the day, and famous for Latin verse; but he was essentially a commonplace don. "Stephen major," he once said to my brother, "if you do not take more pains, how can you ever expect to write good longs and shorts? If you do not write good longs and shorts, how can you ever be a man of taste? If you are not a man of taste, how can you ever hope to be of use in the world?" [8]

In this manner, much of education performs its unique and proper function.

Realistic observation reveals other paradoxes. Anyone who has taught knows that teaching alternates rather unpredictably between moments of exaltation and hours of weariness. Learning occurs by dull practice and in moments of creative insight. The first is manageable; the latter are precarious and fleeting. Both appear to be an integral part of teaching and learning.

The formal, academic study of education reflects the inconsistencies of the subject. It has been an object of systematic inquiry for the greatest intellects and for the most mediocre. From Plato's *Republic* to Dewey's *Democracy and Education*, philosophers have written learned treatises on the subject, and dull men have put into labored volumes their views. All of them have believed in the importance of education and have generally decried the pedantry of the schools. But all of them have come out upon the dry, flat, monotonous plains of pedagogy. Not recognizing

[7] Paul Shorey, *Horace: Odes and Epodes* (Boston: Benjamin H. Sanborn and Company, 1913), p. 176.
[8] Leslie Stephens, *The Life of Sir James Fitzjames Stephen, Bart.* (New York: G. P. Putnam's Sons, 1895), pp. 80–81.

the paradox in their subject, they have often attempted to make education immediately important or to be immediately concerned with intrinsically important ends—"To prepare us for complete living is the function which education has to discharge," said Spencer.[9] The difficulty lies in the fact that the relation of what goes on in the schools and "complete" living is so devious that it can hardly be traced by any methods we know.

The role of the teacher in society also reflects the essential contradiction. He is paid homage, but little money; his profession is honored, but as a person he is thought to be tedious or pathetic. Under the constant scrutiny of the public, he is badgered and pressured by an incredible array of persons and organizations; but personally he remains a stranger, an important but a peripheral and individually an expendable member of society.

Education as Intellectual and Practical

The educational activity includes those studies that are inherently pleasurable intellectually and those that are designated for some practical end. This dualism certainly represents an oversimplification, and it may be spurious. Dewey would abolish it,[10] as would other pragmatists: "Interest in truth for its own sake—the pure and undistracted purpose to know—is not the characteristic purpose of knowing." [11] There are other modern educational philosophers who are equally certain on the other side: "Liberal Education, viewed in itself, is simply the cultivation of the intellect, as such, and its object is nothing more or less than intellectual excellence." [12]

[9] Herbert Spencer, *Education* (New York: D. Appleton and Company, 1896), p. 31.
[10] See Dewey, *Democracy and Education*, Chap. xx.
[11] Clarence Irving Lewis, *An Analysis of Knowledge and Valuation* (LaSalle, Ill.: Open Court Publishing Company, 1945), p. 422.
[12] John Cardinal Newman, *The Idea of a University* (London and New York: Longmans, Green and Company, 1883), p. 121.

Education

Within the schools both kinds of activities persist. The study of analytic geometry, for example, may have no foreseeable practical value, except to show the connection between algebra and geometry, but, notwithstanding its impracticality, it appeals to some students. Likewise, the study of Latin meters, or of the influence of Ennius on Lucretius, would be difficult to justify by practical results. To understand Latin prosody or to be able to recognize literary influences in ancient authors are kinds of knowledge that have scant practical worth. However, both Latin and geometry are still regarded as appropriate educational interests. Appropriate also in educational organizations is the study of engineering, business, typing, medicine, library science, and printing. Professional and vocational subjects are an integral part of the educational enterprise. Because these matters can be taught, and because modern conditions demand that they be taught in organizations, the schools have taken over much of the training that was formerly carried on through apprenticeship.

Education is, therefore, responsible intellectual play and honest practical training. We find in the schools those studies that are impossible to justify on utilitarian grounds and those that are thoroughgoing and authentic in their practical aims. Although they may have their preferences, many, if not most, teachers recognize the validity of the claims of both kinds of education. The familiar quarrel between them is also familial. Education for practical ends has an obvious objective and, in a society fighting for survival, ready public support. Education that offers only intellectual satisfactions is more difficult to justify. Consequently, we find that by sound instinct most educational institutions, and even society itself, pays a kind of homage to the most esoteric intellectual pursuits. Practical education, on the other hand, because of its effective and facile warrants, has often had to endure scathing academic scorn. The distribution of demand for the practical and prestige for the purely intellectual is an expression of educational justice that tends to insure the continuance of both.

Education as Individual and Social

In our democracy, and perhaps in all other societies, education is concerned both for the common welfare and for the development and the personal satisfactions of individuals. The emphasis may vary from time to time, but usually this duality of purpose obtains. Jefferson, for example, looked to education as a means of social, moral, and political progress as well as an aid to personal and professional advancement of individuals.[13] And, ironically, so did the Nazis, and so do all modern totalitarians. Although the nature of the state may vary, education for citizenship is practically universal. At the same time, and again in varying degrees of emphasis, by its very nature education is essentially concerned with the individual, his interests, abilities, and satisfactions.

Now theoretically the schools may emphasize either one of these objectives, and the means thereto, without neglecting the other. One may argue that since an individual's greatest satisfactions are derived from a prosperous and well-ordered society, there is actually no denial of individual rights in requiring each person, not only to be educated for the general responsibilities of citizenship, but even to modify some of his own immediate intellectual and vocational preferences in light of social needs. Conversely, one may say that if each individual pursues his education according to his aptitudes, preferences, and abilities, the variety of talents and tastes existing in the population will automatically provide for the skills, attitudes, and accomplishments that the social order requires. In either case social efficiency and personal culture are synonymous goals for education.

However, the dualism between the individual and society

[13] See Roy J. Honeywell's *The Educational Work of Thomas Jefferson* (Cambridge, Mass.: Harvard University Press, 1931), pp. 146–59.

Education

persists. The dilemma persists,[14] but practice, which cannot wait upon a clear-cut resolution of the conflict, proceeds inconsistently and emphasizes both aims even when they appear to be irreconcilable. The offering of elective courses, testing for interests and preferences, and nondirective counseling testify to the respect for individual objectives. On the other hand, the requirement of courses in social problems, the emphasis on the preparation for a socially useful vocation, and the assiduous attention to social development, reflect the concern for the broader social aims of education.

The schools are pledged to encourage the individual to pursue his intellectual development along the lines most congenial to him, and at the same time they are conscious of an obligation to direct his interests toward preparation for a life that is socially useful. Only by assuming that the pursuit of all individual interests will be socially useful can the two objectives be reconciled, and, even then, the question of degree of social usefulness is likely to arise. For example, the current social and national need for engineers and scientists may prompt educational institutions to attempt to modify individual preferences, or at least to direct them toward a curriculum that obviously fulfills a social need. And in a more general way public policy may demand that we concern ourselves with the talented and the able at the expense of the less gifted, even though our humanitarian instincts rebel.

That the social and individual aims of education are in some degree distinct is indicated by a suggestion for the evaluation of educational organizations. Parsons [15] has proposed that the economic theory of "double interchange" may have some validity for education. An industrial organization produces commodities and in so doing increases purchasing power through the payment of

[14] For a current recognition of the problem, see Jacob W. Getzels, "The Acquisition of Values in School and Society," in *The High School in a New Era* (Chicago: University of Chicago Press, 1958), pp. 146–61.

[15] *Ibid.*, pp. 53–56.

wages and salaries. The schools produce individual changes in students and, at the same time, increase the skills, abilities, and general level of performance in many activities in which the community is interested. The contribution to immediate and remote personal satisfactions may coincide in many instances with the social contribution, but only by extending the concept of the coincidence of the general and the individual good to the degree that it has little practical significance can he say that all changes wrought by education are ultimately, if not simultaneously, important for the individual and for social efficiency. This leaves to education in the schools the task of mediating between the contradictory claims of the society that supports education and also between the social claims and those of the individual, which may be antisocial.

Education as Ethical and Aesthetic

The questions about the educational activity, like those about any other, may be divided into two general categories: those that deal with what is being, or can be, accomplished; and those that deal with what should, or ought, to be done. The first are questions of fact and of relationships; for example, what the schools are teaching, or what results follow specific methods of teaching. The second are only indirectly related to facts or relations; they are questions of value, ultimately unanswerable by fact or relation. At first glance, all questions of the second type appear to be ethical, since they contain the words "ought" or "should." But this appearance may be erroneous. All such questions are not necessarily answered in ethical terms, despite the ethical connotations of the language.

To be sure, education is enormously concerned with ethical and moral matters, but to invoke ethical criteria for all "ought" or "should" questions is to assume that they all come under moral

Education

judgment. Apparently this reasoning is disjunctive: all decisions are either morally right or morally wrong. We may say that in choosing a green rather than a blue binding for a book we are not concerned with "ought" or "should," but we do say that one poem should be taught in preference to another, or that one painting should be selected over another because it is aesthetically preferable. And either because we use the word "should," or because of a prior moral judgment about aesthetic "oughts" and "shoulds," we assume that aesthetic standards have a moral warranty. However, if the teacher insists that the students learn to prefer Rembrant over Holman Hunt, it is difficult to see how this is ultimately an ethical or moral choice. The "should" implicit here is partly an aesthetic and partly an intellectual, not a moral, one. Nor can this distinction be abolished by further analysis that might continue as follows: one should prefer Rembrant over Holman Hunt because the former is capable of giving greater aesthetic pleasure, and it is ethical or moral to prefer it on these grounds.

We may ask on what grounds is the aesthetic preference always subject to ethical or moral judgments. Cannot the aesthetic "should" be as final a mandate as the moral one? It is true that when the aesthetic preference violates a moral one, the former may give way to the latter, but when there is no conflict, the invocation of the moral standard would seem to be superfluous. In education as well as in life there appear to be numerous choices that have no moral sanction.

Whether because of puritanism, utilitarianism, or a rational drive toward simplicity, it appears to be difficult for most people to justify aesthetic choices by purely aesthetic warrants. If, however, we assume that to experience the highest aesthetic pleasures may be morally neither right nor wrong, and only in the broadest and almost meaningless sense subject to the utilitarian standard, then it would seem necessary to consider the "ought" invoked as purely aesthetic.

Art is often considered either an enemy or an ally of morality.

162 Administration and Policy-Making in Education

In order to justify art in ethical terms, one student of aesthetics has forced a distinction between the ethical and the moral:

> One illustration of the complexity of human culture is the fact that art has now been regarded as the symbol and ally of goodness, and now as its enemy. This paradox can, I think, be partly explained by making a distinction between the ethical and the moral point of view regarding conduct. From the one point of view, the good belongs to all free creative acts that look toward growth and happiness of individuals; from the other point of view, it consists in conformity to the law, convention, and custom. . . .[16]

The assumption here that the "good" is ultimately always ethical forces the author to distinguish between two systems, one ethical and one moral, in order to include aesthetics.

It is true that there probably is a greater diversity of opinion about what is beautiful than about what is true or what is morally right, but this fact would not in itself deny the assumption that aesthetic judgments may be warranted ultimately by purely aesthetic standards. Intellectual judgments that are based on the most rigorously determined foundations of empirical truth admit of controversy, and to a greater degree the same is true of moral judgments. Furthermore, all three types of judgments may conflict with one another, and there may be a well-determined order of precedence: the aesthetic may give way to the ethical or the ethical to the intellectual. One may prefer beauty to truth, or morality to beauty. But this kind of choice does mean that one must accept a monism of the true, the beautiful, and the good.

The most cursory observation of the classroom will reveal that the teacher is concerned daily with intellectual, moral, and aesthetic matters. However, the literature on the last is scant indeed. The only volume that has been published in the United States is DeGarmo's *Aesthetic Education*,[17] and he introduced

---

[16] DeWitt H. Parker, *Principles of Aesthetics* (New York: P. S. Crofts, 1946), pp. 271-72.
[17] Charles DeGarmo, *Aesthetic Education* (Syracuse: C. W. Bardeen, 1913). In Europe Schiller wrote a series of letters in "The Aesthetic Education of Man," and E. Weber wrote *Aesthetik als pädagogische Grundwissen-*

Education

the subject by saying that the purpose of aesthetic education is the acquisition by every child of an aesthetic view of the world, as he now acquires an intellectual and ethical view. The reasons for the neglect of this aspect of education in the literature need not concern us here, but it may be that the aesthetic has been included in the ethical or the socially useful, perhaps to the extent of inhibiting aesthetic development. Better, perhaps, the principle of *de gustibus* than the moral and intellectual suffocation of innocent aesthetic pleasure; but, since the teacher can no more follow this principle than he can adopt a *laissez-faire* attitude toward intellectual and moral concerns, we are forced to recognize the place of aesthetics in education.

To admit the distinction between moral and aesthetic concerns in education, which seems necessary, is to increase further the variety and pluralism of the standards by which the school may be judged. Also, by introducing the matter of aesthetic judgments it increases the kinds of factually unwarrantable value decisions that must be made. By public will, education is obviously concerned with aesthetic values, but there seems to be a public reluctance to admit that the expenditure of limited means can be justified on purely aesthetic grounds. Therefore the tendency is great to invoke intellectual, moral, or utilitarian warrants even when they do not apply. For example, the teaching of literature and art may be justified by claims of their contribution to citizenship, morality, or intellectual discipline. While these claims may have wide validity, it is possible that their exclusive application may inhibit the attainment of the desired aesthetic ends.

Education as Routine and Creative

Learning has been the object of considerable scientific inquiry, and teaching of no less considerable, but considerably less

---

schaft, 2 Aufl. (Leipzig, 1926). See also, Sir Herbert Read's *Education through Art* (New York, 1945).

scientific, investigation. The conditions that facilitate some kinds of learning are reasonably well known, and some of them can be controlled; but in a large measure the learning process seems to be responsive only to the grossest manipulation of these factors. Teaching, on the other hand, is more controllable than learning; it proceeds by plan and is subject to direct observation. But it too has some unpredictable and surprising aspects. The relationship between teaching and learning need not concern us here, but we are concerned with the fact that both, in varying degrees, are dependent upon activities that are rational, predictable, and controllable and on those that are apparently uncontrollable, unpredictable, and mysterious. Observation of education in the classroom will reveal that a great deal of instruction is carried on in a routine fashion, carefully controlled, directed toward well-defined ends, and on budgeted time and resources. Many of the so-called fundamentals are taught in this way. For example, in teaching the multiplication tables the optimum spacing of drill has been fairly well determined, and, although in simple practice of this kind there are concomitant learnings that are not planned and may not be desired, in a large measure the instruction and the results are fairly consonant. Probably a great deal of teaching can be routinized and even mechanized profitably.

If we take a somewhat more complicated and less clear-cut objective, that of teaching students to solve certain types of intellectual problems, we still find a high degree of planning for the class. Examples are selected ahead of time and procedures are outlined step by step. But, despite Dewey's rationalization of the steps in a complete act of thought, we have no conclusive empirical evidence that actual problem-solving follows any one pattern of mental activity. On the contrary, there is some evidence that there is a great variety in the patterns of thinking in problem-solving.[18] An unpredictable stage of trial and error may be necessary before students find their way to the solutions of

[18] See Guy T. Buswell's *Patterns of Thinking in Problem Solving* (Berkeley and Los Angeles: University of California Press, 1956).

problems, and the steps toward the solutions fall into a great variety of patterns. The classroom activity here cannot be rigidly planned, and instruction cannot profitably follow a prearranged routine. The schedule must be adjusted to the unforeseen turn of events, and the regular class periods may be too brief to accomplish the ends or too long, continuing after the objective has been attained. To be sure, the sensitive and experienced teacher knows the general repertoire of responses and the alternate courses that the thinking and discussion will be likely to take, but the instruction cannot be completely organized. Inevitably the teacher comes to rely on a kind of intuitive knowledge about how, under unique combinations of circumstances, he should encourage and elicit desirable reactions.

Similarly in a lecture, in which the teacher is developing a thesis that is carefully and logically arranged, he will inevitably become sensitive to the silent responses of students, see new implications, and often arrive at new and unexpected conclusions. Likewise in a seminar, which allows for free and rigorous probing of ideas, precise scheduling is difficult, and certainly the results cannot be predicted or measured.

Creative work in both the arts and sciences is distinguished by the appearance of disorganization. By all meaningful standards, efficiency is impossible, disorder inevitable, and prearranged schedules rarely coterminous with optimum conditions. Here the teacher must rely exceedingly on unknown and unpredictable factors: the creative impulses of the students, his own intuitive judgment about how to release these powers, and the final surprising quality of products of creative efforts. The teacher may provide the general environment that he believes to be conducive to creative work, lavish encouragement, and an element of discipline, but he cannot successfully set rigid procedures and schedules. The imagination at work, when it can be observed, is often unseemly and chaotic. It may even appear ridiculous until the magic of synthesis weaves a sublime pattern: "Chaos precedes cosmos, and it is into chaos without form and void that we have plunged." [19] It is this chaos that provides the milieu of education.

There may be a tacit assumption on the part of most students of teaching and learning that all the conditions that produce learning are capable of being known. If this is so, theoretically it would be possible to provide these conditions so that the unpredictability of the results may be eliminated or at least reduced. Progress in this direction is highly desirable from both a practical and an intellectual view. However, this assumption does not allow for a possible free, creative, random element in learning that is not amenable to any kind of scheduling. For the present, we can operate only on the best evidence that we have, and it indicates clearly that while many kinds of educational and intellectual activity may be routinized, for others routine may be inhibiting or impossible. The question in education is not whether or not it is entirely a determinate enterprise, but rather it is what to do about the indeterminate components in human thought and behavior.

Summary

The educational activity appears to be extremely varied both as to ends and means. Whatever the reason for this diversity, whether it resides in the nature of education, in the primitive state of our knowledge, or in the idiosyncrasies of teachers, it calls for a pluralism of institutions, curriculums, and methods. Moreover, the enterprise seems to be shot through with paradoxes; ultimately of the greatest importance, education must be justified frequently by immediate trivialities or extremely remote and intangible consequences. Dependent on the creative intellect, as well as on the routine procedures for habituation, it apparently can be organized

[19] John Livingston Lowes, *The Road to Xanadu* (Boston: Houghton-Mifflin Company, 1930), p. 12.

only in part. Subject to the claims of both the individual and society, it must mediate between them. And concerned with both fact and values, it must invoke a variety of warrants to justify its means. Its institutionalization has brought this strangely varied activity into intimate contact with the necessities of organization. The ensuing relationship we propose to examine in the next chapter.

CHAPTER IX

Administration and education

IN AN ESSAY entitled "The Twentieth Century Bureaucrat" Rebecca West has clearly distinguished between two levels of interpretation of the rather mysterious writings of Kafka:

> For these books [*The Trial* and *The Castle*] are on one level about bureaucracy as "Hamlet" is on one level about the affairs of the royal family of Elsinore, though on a deeper level they are, like "Hamlet," about the soul of man and his prospects of salvation and damnation.[1]

However, despite her perceptive interpretation of both levels of meaning, Miss West leaves the problem of the relation between bureaucracy and the soul of man as enigmatic as ever. In some ways it is a relation of conflict; bureaucracy and the spirit of individual man are mutually antagonistic. In an infinitely more prosaic vein we have attempted to describe the conditions under which this conflict occurs in the schools, where administrative

[1] Rebecca West, *The Court and the Castle* (New Haven: Yale University Press, 1957), p. 282. The essay was published also as "Kafka and the Mystery of Bureaucracy," *Yale Review*, Autumn, 1957, p. 17.

Administration and Education

bureaucracy and intensive individual pursuits stand in an intimate relation. It now remains for us to inquire into the manner of this relation.

First, however, we shall try to add to the clarity of the distinction between the administrative and educational strata within the organization. The principal source of confusion seems to be the fact that administrative officials at every level in the hierarchy allegedly possess technical qualifications for the aspect or level of education that they administer. Thus, the assistant superintendent of schools, in charge of secondary education, a "line" official, may be regarded as a specialist in secondary education, rather than, or at least as much as, an administrator of a branch of the educational system. Weber foresaw that the increasing number of positions that required specialized knowledge would enhance the growth of bureaucracy.[2] It is our theory that the course bureaucracy has taken now makes necessary a distinction between two kinds of technical knowledge and the ways in which they are used in organizations. A person who occupies a position at any given point in the hierarchy, for example, the assistant superintendent in charge of secondary education, has some responsibility for the technical and professional operations in his department, bureau, division, branch, or section; but due to the increase of purely organizational demands, he is forced into devoting most of his time to activities we have classified as administrative. In other words, the bureaucrat tends to practice his managerial specialty.

At the same time, because of the increase of specialization, the intrinsic functions of many organizations, and particularly of educational organizations, demand greater technical knowledge. For example, at a time in the not so remote past, one man could be a teacher of physics, Latin, and history, and also principal or

---

[2] "The Essentials of Bureaucratic Organization: An Ideal Type of Construction," in *Reader in Bureaucracy*, Robert K. Merton, Ailsa P. Gray, Barbara Hockey, and Hanon C. Selvin, eds. (Glencoe, Ill.: The Free Press of Glencoe, Illinois, 1952), pp. 18–27.

administrator of the school; but today the intrinsic activities of the school have become more specialized in their subject matter, and clearer distinction is possible between teaching and administering. In effect, then, in the school organization we are seeing the emergence of two specialized classes: bureaucrats who have a heavy responsibility for administration and "professionals" who are concerned with both the content and method of the technical or intrinsic functions.[3] This distinction appears in government agencies, hospitals, churches, research institutions, and other organizations in which the intrinsic activities require specialized knowledge, creativity, contemplation, and individual control over the methods and conditions of practice. Certainly it is not always clear; many individuals continue to act at both levels, and even when the separation is obvious, many administrative officials are reluctant to relinquish their former "professional" role.

This distinction between the two types of activities within the educational organization suggests questions about the relations between them. The final proposition of our general theory of educational administration, which is derived from our assumptions about the nature of administration and of education, postulates the general character of their relation. This proposition is:

> Administration, which is essential to the maintenance and survival of all organizations, varies in its degree of compatibility with the several intrinsic functions of organizations; and this incompatibility varies in inverse order to the degree of specialization, creativity, and individuality necessary to perform them.

Assuming that administration as we have defined it remains constant in its nature, we should expect it to attain a maximum degree of compatibility with intrinsic organizational functions that lead to predictable consequences that are matter of fact,

---

[3] A similar distinction is made in Arnold M. Rose's " 'Official' vs. 'Administrative' Criteria for Classification of Combat Breakdown Cases," *Administrative Science Quarterly*, III (September, 1958), 185–94. More appropriate nomenclature might be "Professional" and "Administrative."

Administration and Education

amenable to scheduling, routine, and warrantable by immediate, quantitative, and utilitarian standards. Conversely, we should expect to find a minimum degree of compatibility with intrinsic organizational functions that are creative, contemplative, and highly individual, or which have remote and intangible objectives. For example, in an automobile assembly plant, administration and the intrinsic activity would appear to operate with a maximum degree of harmony, whereas in the design department of an automobile manufacturing company, we can expect less compatibility between the two. And in the Art Students League, administration, which serves the organization, such as it is, would be likely to conflict seriously with the essential activity of producing art and artists. From what we know—and what we do not know—about education, it is logical to assume that it falls somewhere between these two extremes: some aspects of it are quite harmonious with the administrative necessities of organization, and others are greatly at variance.

Education and Administrative Discernment of Purpose

Not only does administration appear to vary in its compatibility with different aspects of education, but the different aspects of administration may vary in this regard also. The first responsibility of administration, that of discerning the purposes of an organization through an accurate and objective interpretation of the will of the policy-making bodies, may hold fewer possibilities of conflict than the other aspects of administration, partly because it is restricted in large measure to the upper level of administration. However, there is one obvious source of conflict: in the discernment of purpose, administration is forced to look outside the organization, to become conscious of a wide range of social needs, and to hearken to lay opinion; while on the other hand, the intrinsic function of the educational organization depends largely on the specialized, intensely personal, and somewhat cloistered outlook of the academician or intellectual.

We do not propose here to enter into a discussion of the merits of leaving the determination of over-all policy-making for educational organizations to lay boards of control, the legislatures, and the courts. This is the situation that prevails in the United States. Administration, therefore, stands between the prudent, practical, normal, confident world outside and the specialized, reflective, esoteric academic world within. It must conform to the world outside, not to every pressure group, to be sure, but to the prevailing systems of values and the current social needs. It must be responsive to a broad range of interests, often local, often immediate, often opportunistic. The administrator, therefore, is open to the charge of servility to the outside community with its alleged conservatism, provincialism, philistinism, and anti-intellectualism.

The educational activity is dependent to some degree for its success upon specialized, personal interests that are related often only remotely and obscurely to the social demands for the schools. In the presence of administrative powers and responsibilities, these interests may be extremely uneasy. They are devoted to an ideal that, although narrow and restricted, may well extend beyond the obvious values of the community that supports the organization. For example, the fellowship of mathematicians may have a narrow and esoteric set of values, but it is an international fellowship. Furthermore, academic interests may not coincide with immediate social needs, which are always the most urgent; the countercyclical aspect of education also brings it into disagreement with administration. Confined by the narrowness of their classrooms and laboratories, devoted to academic ideals that may have only a remote relation to social needs, and involved in the intricacies of their subjects, academic personnel at all levels of education, and particularly at the higher levels, where the curriculum deviates progressively from the curriculum of life, are uneasy about the compromises administration must make with immediate social needs.[4]

We may expect, therefore, the uncommitted, reconciling, pragmatic approach to the discernment of original and changing purposes of the educational organization to come into conflict with the imaginative, devoted, narrow interests of the teacher, the scholar, and the artist.[5] The administrators are often regarded as unimaginative, stifling Philistines, who by their compromise and improvisation violate the sanctity of academic ideals. The academicians are in turn seen as irresponsible, unrealistic prima donnas, narrow, Bohemian, and unpredictable. Between the administrative function of discerning organizational purposes and the stratum of academic activity, a tension seems inevitable. It is only one point of conflict between the two, a conflict that, we believe, is inherent in the respective natures of their work.

Education and Co-ordination

Through the co-ordinating function, administration comes into intimate relations with education. We have assumed (1) that because of its increasing size and complexity, education must be carried on in formal organizations; (2) that organization depends upon co-ordination, i.e., upon the directing of the various activities within the organization in their reciprocal relations in such a way that they contribute maximally toward the attainment of the organization's purposes; and (3) that certain aspects of education are inhibited and interfered with by this very co-ordination

[4] For a fictional portrayal of this conflict, see C. P. Snow's *The New Men* (New York: Charles Scribner's Sons, 1954).
[5] For a clear recognition of this difference, see Ross L. Mooney, *Meeting Cultural Blocks to Creativity in the Army Engineer Research and Development Laboratories* (Columbus: Bureau of Educational Research, The Ohio State University, 1957).

that enables an educational organization to survive. At this point we are not interested in resolving this conflict, but merely in showing how it follows from our general theory of administration and how this assumption throws light on some of the problems in education.

In order to show how this conflict arises in an organization, we shall give examples from hypothetical, but we trust realistic, educational situations. First, let us look at a high school schedule, the visible structure of co-ordination. In the words of one authority on the subject, the daily schedule "prescribes the time, place, personnel and general facilities for the educative experiences which are accepted and promoted by the high school."[6] The schedule must provide a time and place for each class and each teacher; and it must also provide them in such a way that they do not interfere with one another. Scheduling thus becomes a major co-ordinating task and an extremely important one for a large high school with a comprehensive and varied curriculum. The administrator must know all the activities to be scheduled and have as much information as possible about their respective requirements for time, space, and materials. However, in the actual scheduling, when the individual requirements conflict irreconcilably with the over-all demands of the organization, the latter must be given preference. Conflicts, chaos, and confusion are evidences of poor administration. Administration, therefore, strives to reduce the evidence against itself. In the last analysis the daily schedule is the best compromise available among the demands and possibilities of the subject to be scheduled. The minimum compromise is likely to be made by the organization itself.

In the schedule it is usually necessary in order to avoid conflict to arrange for each class to meet regularly and for the same length of time each day. Only in this way can a workable apportionment of time be given to all subjects. Some types of education are certainly amenable to this kind of scheduling. From what we know

[6] R. Emerson Langfitt, *The Daily Schedule and High School Organization* (New York: The Macmillan Company, 1938), p. 1.

about drill, for example, it is possible to provide optimum conditions by regular periods. However, there are other kinds of techniques in education that probably require a much more flexible organization. In the creative arts, in research, in the solution of problems, it is not always possible to predict the optimum length of a class period. On some occasions a class fifteen minutes in length may be sufficient to show that a longer period would be a waste of time; on others a half day at least may be required to accomplish without interruption the objectives of an assignment. But since these occasions cannot be predicted with accuracy, concessions are made to the demands of the organization as a whole. Furthermore, in order to obtain uniformity in educational practices, standardized procedures in scheduling have been adopted. Quantitative units and credits become symbols for regular quantities of time. For example, the Carnegie unit, fifteen or sixteen of which are required for high school graduation, is based on a forty-five-minute period for five days each week. By this technique, the institutions of education acquired a smoothness and a glaze that reduces interorganizational friction.

Recognition of the regimentation brought on by scheduling has not been lacking in the literature on educational administration. Modifications of the rigid, conventional plans are being recommended.[7] However, if our theory of the unpredictability of the time schedules required for some aspects of education is correct, it is difficult to see how administration can plan schedules in complex organizations flexible enough to be modified abruptly on the basis of the fitful demands of the immediate situation in one class without interfering with the work being done in other classes.

Another example of the inherent conflict between co-ordination and education can be taken from the modern university, where diverse types of educational activities are carried on. Teaching,

[7] See, for example, Will French, J. Dan Hull, and B. L. Dodds, *American High School Administration* (New York: Rinehart and Company, 1957), Chap. XII and XIII, pp. 271–307.

research, consulting, community service, creative and artistic endeavor are all means for the accomplishment of the organization's purposes. The co-ordination of a variety of disciplines within each one of these activities, and of the various activities themselves, demands administrative machinery at all levels to reduce interference and conflict. Arrangements must continually be made so that these activities will not conflict with one another; and the enforcement of these arrangements may well impede and dishearten many of the intrinsic activities of the organization. Evidence that this is so is not conclusive, but there is reason to question the record of organizations to produce innovations, and to foster inventive, original, and creative pursuits.[8] Independence of judgment, a tendency to "waste" time on new and impractical ideas, an impatience with consensus and easy order, and a willingness to face the fact that he is at odds with the common sense of his community appear to characterize the creative scholar.[9] For the sake of the organization that it is obliged to maintain, administration inevitably exhibits a limited tolerance for these traits.

The inescapable irony in this situation lies in the fact that the administrative function that is designed to prevent the divers activities within an organization from interfering with one another itself provides interference for some of them. One answer that may be expected is that the organization with its attendant administration should be subservient to all the intrinsic functions. Organization, say those who propose this solution, is actually as well as etymologically a tool; and if it is not conducive in every respect to the accomplishment of the educational task, it should be modified so that it will be.[10] Administration should serve. But this answer overlooks the facts that there are few, if any, perfect

[8] See, for example, John Jewkes, David Somers, and Richard Stillerman, *The Sources of Invention* (London: The Macmillan Company, 1958).
[9] See Frank Barron, "The Psychology of Imagination," *Scientific American*, cxix (September, 1958), 151 ff.; also J. P. Guilford, "Creativity," *The American Psychologist*, v (September, 1950), 444–54.
[10] See Friedrich Schneider, "Organization und Erziehung," *Internationale Zietschrift für Erziehungswissenschaft*. Fünfter Jahrgang, Zweites Heft 1918/19, pp. 149–60.

tools; that all tools have their deficiencies as well as their advantages; and that the tool that is necessary for the conduct of education may also be harmful in some respects.

To digress for the moment from educational organization, we find a lively concern over our alleged conflict between organizational conformity on one hand and ingenuity and creativity on the other among reflective business administrators. Management's resistance to change is regarded as a barrier to creativity; [11] flexible organization is deemed essential for the dissenter, the lone wolf, and the pure experimenter to make their contributions; [12] and autonomy of the individual over his own methods of operation, whenever possible, is recommended.[13] If business administrators exhibit so grave a concern over these matters, we should expect educational administrators, who have made "creative teaching" a cliche, to be genuinely alarmed. Perhaps their fears in this regard are balanced by a love of stability and by a traditional belief that excessive intellectualism and creativity will disrupt the foundations of order. They may be right. But in their immediate and urgent responsibility for the well-being of organization, *qua* organization, they may easily sacrifice the intrinsic function to facile administrative success.

We do not wish to leave the impression that we believe that all educational and intellectual pursuits are hindered by the scheduling, the regularity, and the group effort of organizations. Many, perhaps most, aspects of such pursuits are enhanced and encouraged by some discipline imposed by administrative arrangement and direction, to say nothing of the necessary physical resources that only an organization can provide. And only the most conspicuously immature and unco-operative scholar or teacher will claim that the meeting of reasonable schedules always inter-

[11] Leo B. Moore, in *Company Climate and Creativity* (New York: Deutsch and Shea, Industrial Relations News, 1959), p. 38.
[12] W. John Upjohn in *Creativity*, Paul Smith, ed. (New York: Hastings House, 1959), pp. 173–78.
[13] Crawford H. Greenewalt, *The Uncommon Man* (New York: McGraw-Hill Book Company, 1959), pp. 26–28.

feres with his imagination and creative impulses. Many unquestionably depend upon the regular schedules set by administrators to get the work done. However, there does appear to be here an irreconcilable antagonism between administration and some aspects of the educational enterprise.

Education and Public Relations

Public relations, the third aspect of the administrative process, we have defined as the effort to obtain material and moral support for the educational organization. Since the material means for the support of all the organizations society has created are not unlimited, considerable competition is inevitable for the available funds. Educational organizations must compete with other organizations that have more urgent claims to the public purse. Furthermore, some phases of the intrinsic functions of educational organizations, particularly those that lead indirectly and remotely to the accomplishment of their purposes, are difficult to support. It is true that administration through its public relations aspect is responsible for obtaining support for all the accepted purposes of education, but because some of the intrinsic activities of the organization are so remotely and inefficiently related to the attainment of these purposes, it is difficult to obtain adequate support for them. Since administrators cannot but be interested in their own success, they are likely to be partial to their aspects of education that are the best subjects for obtaining public support. This fact may tend to discourage the vigorous pursuit of important but unsalable educational activities.

Not only may some important phases of the intrinsic functions of educational organizations be unsalable, but they may also detract from the support of the organization. Powerful minority groups may object to certain activities, procedures, or personnel that are essential to the educational enterprise and withdraw or interfere with public support. Again, the administrator, whose success will be measured immediately by the prosperity of the organization, will be tempted to accede to the influences that directly affect his success.

In organizations that lead a precarious existence, and most educational organizations do, the temptation is great for administrations to concentrate on those activities that are easiest to support. The financially popular enterprises within the organization may enjoy administrative favor, although they may not be the most important for the attainment of the accepted purposes of the organization. In universities struggling to survive, basic research may have to limp along on limited budgets, and in the schools the so-called "frills" such as art may be inadequately supported. Administration, which tends to be "success-minded" and, perhaps, must be so, will be likely to maintain little tolerance for such activities as compared with those that are "useful."

Administrators at all levels of education realize the need for unrestricted funds. They realize that even when all the purposes of an organization have been clearly accepted, the financial support, even though it is sufficient for the accomplishment of these purposes, is not always apportioned according to the necessities of the various intrinsic activities. In the allocation of funds on a basis other than the attractiveness of the intrinsic activities for financial support lies a whole area of administrative discretion. But this discretion can operate only after the funds have been obtained. It is in the solicitation of support that administration is likely to discriminate against those aspects of the intrinsic function of their organizations that, although important, are not obviously related to the accomplishment of immediate organizational objectives, or are otherwise difficult to "sell."

Other Sources of Conflict

There are other sources of conflict over the differences in values, or rather the emphases on values, between administrators and academicians; and there are different types of personalities attracted to the respective tasks within an organization. We have already shown that the educational administrator, by virtue of his responsibilities, is more likely to hold the general values of society, and in somewhat the same hierarchy, than are teachers, scholars, artists, and intellectuals in general. One of the values that holds a disputed rank is efficiency. For administration, efficiency does not mean mere effectiveness, but rather the maximization of results with the minimum of resources.[14] For an organization to accomplish its objectives with as little expenditure of time, energy, and money as possible is an administrative desideratum. Even in those organizations that are designed to spend and distribute wealth, such as some of the government agencies during the depression, administration almost inevitably had to invoke this criterion for its own success. Also, efficiency is a value generally and highly held.

Academic personnel, on the other hand, are not likely to give efficiency as high a rank as administrators. Particularly is this so when to invoke it might threaten to inhibit or jeopardize the activity in which they are engaged. Better in their minds to be prodigal with means and to fail in efficiency, than to take the chance of failing in the intrinsic activity in order to succeed administratively.

This criterion of efficiency, which adminstration apparently must invoke, can be applied with dubious validity to the whole of the educational activity. In educational organizations, it is always possible to account for the money spent; it is not always possible to measure the results. Although all administrative decisions are made on the basis of their efficacy to achieve certain ends—facts with values attached—it is often impossible to determine what has been accomplished. Some of the results of administrative acts in education can be rather accurately measured, but many cannot

---

[14] For an excellent discussion of efficiency in administration, see Herbert A. Simon, *Administrative Behavior* (New York: The Macmillan Company, 1953), Chap. IX, pp. 172–97.

as yet be expressed in measurable terms. Simon stresses the great need for and the magnitude of a research program to define the values or objectives of social institutions in terms that permit their observation and measurement under both administrative and extra-administrative variables.[15] Theoretically, observation and measurement would reveal facts, the values of which are determined ultimately by popular preference.

Now the degree of accomplishment of most, if not all, the objectives of educational organization is theoretically objectively measurable—hence, perhaps, the use of the word objective. While the values attached may not be, at least the facts are; and also it is theoretically possible to determine whether the values are preferred. But to say that the facts are theoretically ascertainable does not mean that practically it can be done. One of the objectives of church schools may well be to prepare the students for the life everlasting. Theoretically, it is possible to know how well this has been done, but not until the evaluator has reluctantly shambled off the mortal coil can he be sure, and even then there is no satisfactory way to communicate the results. Even with some less remote objectives, both in time and place, the problems of phrasing these objectives in measurable, behavioral terms, and of controlling all variables, are extremely difficult.

On the other hand, it is comparatively easy to compute the costs, particularly the financial ones. It can be shown how many students must pay tuition for a course in order that the organization meet the expense. Other and more important courses as far as the purposes of the organization are concerned may have to be offered at a deficit. Since their consequences may not show up until long after the end of the fiscal year, and then in remote places and unrecognizable forms, the temptation is for administration to make decisions on the basis of a tangible, understandable, and generally acceptable criterion, that of a complete accounting of the financial input and output, accompanied of necessity by only a very fragmentary evaluation of the educational results. Ob-

[15] *Ibid.*, p. 189.

viously, efficiency is necessarily high in the hierarchy of administrative values, and obviously, also, it has serious limitations when applied to education.

We shall mention another probable source of tension between administration and education; it is the difference in the temperaments of the people attracted to the two levels of organizational life. It is reasonable to expect the practical, publicly exalted enterprise of administration to appeal to temperaments that are at ease with the consequences of their own decisions, to the prudent, responsible, methodical, decisive men who can carry out an idea or a policy. Teaching, scholarship, and creative intellectual pursuits, on the other hand, would be more likely to appeal to the more irresolute, the more contemplative, the more unrealistic, to the Tonio Krögers, who are given to brooding uncertainty and intellectual complexities. The former type tends to make all problems concrete and manageable, or at least to devote his energies to the ones that are; the latter to complicate the simplest problem by inquiring and imagining beyond the limits of practical necessity. Certainly, this classification does not apply universally, but it is probable that persons of the temperaments described above do seek to be placed or drift into these respective positions. Also, we must face the possibility that noncreative persons engaged in the intrinsic function of the educational organization may inhibit the more creative ones.

A final observation continues this sense of the irreconcilable. Weber conceived of bureaucracy as a form of rationalization and as a step forward in the *Entzauberung* of the world.[16] Now *Entzauberung* means "disenchantment," and the bureaucrat is probably as little enchanted with the world as anyone. Also, he is rational in that he proceeds on the assumption that by reason and practical intelligence, workable, if not correct, solutions may be found for all problems. He does not seek new problems; rather he devises workable solutions to the ones he has. The scholar, on

[16] Carl J. Friedrich, "Some Observations on Weber's Analysis of Bureaucracy," in *Reader in Bureaucracy*, p. 27.

Administration and Education

the other hand, pursues the irritating role of questioning acceptable answers and of creating new and more complex problems for their own sake. Likewise, the artist continues to be enchanted with experience; he restores the mystery the bureaucrat dispels; and he refuses to become predictable. The institutions of education must contain somehow the reasonable bureaucrat, the restless scholar, and the enchanted artist.

If our description of this conflict is a true picture of organizational life, most administrators, and perhaps most readers who are interested in administration, will immediately begin to think of a practical solution. If, by chance, a "scholar" reads these assumptions, he would be expected to probe the matter further, to find inconsistencies in the theory, to enjoy the distractions, and to draw logical conclusions. Although it may disappoint both kinds of readers, we propose neither to work out carefully a practical solution nor to pursue the logic of our system further. However, in the next and final chapter, one will find a few suggestions that are designed to appease both the seeker of practical solutions and the tireless pursuer of "truth."

CHAPTER X

Implications for research and practice

THE GENERAL THEORY of educational administration that has been formulated may be subjected to a variety of judgments. This statement should occasion no surprise, since in the beginning we defined theory in such a way as to include most, if not all, forms of reflective thinking. But even if this were not so, if on the contrary we had limited our definition of theory to a statement of relationships, or of causes, it would still be true that our theory could be judged in several different ways.

At one extreme there are purely formal criteria: Is the theory consistent internally? Does it possess the elegance of simplicity? Although there may be some question about what is logical and what is not, logical consistency is invariably a virtue in a theory. Simplicity in theory is valued not only for its practical consequences, but many philosophers and scientists profess to derive great aesthetic enjoyment from economy of assumption: "As it is, its [the heliocentric theory] marvelous simplicity furnishes many with an aesthetic enjoyment unequaled in human experience." [1]

[1] Laurence Buermeyer, et al., An Introduction to Reflective Thinking (Boston: Houghton-Mifflin Company, 1923), p. 60.

Implications for Research and Practice

We do not propose to examine the assumptions about the nature of beauty that are implicit in this statement—probably they are similar to those behind Edna St. Vincent Millay's:

> Euclid alone
> Has looked on Beauty bare.

But whether simplicity is aesthetic or not, it is often applied in the judgment of a theory.

At the other extreme, there is the practical, common-sense criterion that is invoked to determine whether or not a theory corresponds to reality, whether it mirrors the world, whether it resembles fact. In this kind of judgment we do not ask whether a theory is correct, simple, or elegant, but whether it is true. And the most common way of proving whether or not a theory is true is by comparing it with the world, or rather with our experience of the world.

In between these two extremes there are other and more complicated criteria. For example, a theory, for reasons of convenience and efficiency, should reduce the number of explanations required for an increasing number of phenomena. Or, if a theory does not lend itself immediately to the tests of truth, it should be fertile as a source of hypotheses that are empirically testable. Also, at a very sophisticated level, a theory may be judged as to whether or not it may lead to the discovery of phenomena that are not discernible by direct observation. And even though a theory does not meet any of the standards indicated above, it may be original, interesting, or historically important.

In this chapter, we propose to point out a few of the possibilities for judging and testing the theory that has been formulated in the preceding pages and to indicate some of its implications for practice. Since ultimately it will stand or fall on its correspondence to empirical fact, it should be possible to deduce testable hypotheses from the general propositions stated. However, it is to be hoped that the general theory will be judged in other ways. Even if it fails all other tests, it may still retain some historical importance if it stimulates theories of educational administration that prove to be more correct and more in accord with the world of administration as we experience it.

Possibilities for Research

The first proposition in this general theory made two assertions: (1) administration can be identified and unambiguously defined; and (2) it is essentially the same activity in all organizations. These assertions were developed in a chapter devoted to definition. The first part of our definition was taken arbitrarily from the dictionaries and the definitions in common use. Now a lexical definition is always a description of a usage and a form of history; as such it is capable of being submitted to verification. The first question to be asked is: Does the definition given here correspond to the one the lexicographers gave the word? Thus, the first and least exciting test involves reading the dictionaries. However, one may in turn attempt to find out whether or not the dictionary definition corresponds to the way in which the word is, or has been, used in speech and writing.

Our definition went beyond both the mere lexical and the definitions in common use. After we attempted to determine what part of the dictionary and common usage definitions seemed to be agreed upon, we sought to find out what part of the partial definitions, i.e., those possessing some, but lacking universal, acceptance, could be said to be implicit in the common one; or, to phrase the question another way; Can the common definition be extended logically to include the variable parts of definitions? For example, we accepted the common definition that administration is the execution or the carrying out of over-all policy or organizational purposes; consequently, the adoption or modification of these purposes would not logically belong to administration. If it were practically impossible to carry out purposes without modifying them, then the definition of administration should be changed to correspond to a possibility. If we assert, quite logically, that administration is obliged to engage in the solicitation of public support for an organization in order that it may survive and accomplish its accepted purposes, then we cannot logically include the soliciting of support for a change in an organization's objectives. More rigorous analytical and logical treatment than we have been able to give would probably reduce the ambiguity that remains. There is probably an unavoidable stipulative element involved here that is impossible to verify, because the writer simply tells the reader how he proposes to use the word. It is possible, however, to determine whether or not the author uses the word in the way that he indicates.[2]

There are other ways in which our definition of administration may be tested. If the words of the definition, which the philosophers call the definiens, are not in a more familiar vocabulary than the word to be defined—the definiendum—there is no gain in clarity. Or a definition may be tautological, and although this condition may not destroy its value completely, it may prevent any gain, and it does offend against both logic and language. For stipulative definitions, there are several recognized rules.[3] For example, the definition should not change the emotional force of the word. From the lack of clarity, precision, and honest style in much of the literature of the social sciences, it would appear that some, not necessarily abject, humility before words as they are used in definitions would be helpful.

Following our analytical procedure further, we defined administration as consisting of three distinct activities: (1) the discernment of an organization's purposes; (2) the direction of the internal affairs within an organization in their reciprocal relations and toward the accomplishment of these purposes; and (3) public relations in the sense of obtaining material and moral

[2] See Richard Robinson, *Definition* (Oxford: The Clarendon Press, 1950), p. 35.
[3] *Ibid.*, pp. 80–92.

support for an organization. Obviously there are hazards involved in a taxonomy of this kind, but there are also evidences of its value, and there are safeguards. First, although we can never say that these activities are "really" administration, we can, as has already been indicated, determine whether or not they are logically implicit in the definition; and, with more precise phrasing, one can test empirically whether or not these are the principal activities—both in terms of time spent in, and the effect of these activities, or the lack of it on, an organization—that persons commonly called administrators perform in their official positions. It is obvious that they are not the principal activities of a teacher, an electrician, or a novelist. Careful recording and classification of the activities of educational administrators, with some concern for reliability by increasing the number of observers, would reveal the nature of the work educational administrators do.

To test our theory at this point there is a need for systematic observation and classification. Some students of administration have made promising suggestions [4] for techniques that may be applied to test the extension of our theory that the administrative process is the same in all organizations. In addition to the capture and record techniques, which would reveal the similarities [5]—or lack of them—in the function that is called administration in all organizations, case studies of what happens when administrators are interchanged among organizations might be made. Although the practice is unknown in public education, there are numerous instances of industrial, governmental, or military administrators being assigned to institutions of higher education and to a lesser extent, perhaps, of college and university presidents assuming administrative positions in other types of organizations.

[4] See, for example, Sune Carlson, *Executive Behaviour* (Stockholm, Sweden: C. A. Stromberg Aktiebolag, 1951). Reprinted in part in *Reader in Bureaucracy*, Robert K. Merton, Ailsa P. Gray, Barbara Hockey, and Hanon C. Selvin, eds. (Glencoe, Ill.: The Free Press of Glencoe, Illinois, 1952), pp. 430–38.

[5] Paul Malcolm Allen, *The Administrative Process: A Comparative Study of Educational and Business Administration* (University of Michigan, Ann Arbor), unpublished doctoral dissertation.

Implications for Research and Practice

Perhaps the most controversial among the many assumptions made in this general theory of educational administration is the one that clearly separates the administrative function from that of deciding what the purposes or the over-all policy of the educational organization should be. That administrators do not, either explicitly or inadvertently and inevitably, modify purposes in the execution of the purposes is a major foundation stone in our theory. If they do, then our theory suffers a shattering but not necessarily completely devastating blow. It is important, therefore, to suggest at least how this assumption may be tested.

The original organization to which our theory applies is the American educational system. Simon has pointed out that "A democratic state is committed to popular control over these value elements, and the distinction of value from fact is of basic importance in securing a proper relation between policy making and administration." [6] If we assume that the purposes of the educational organization consist of the accomplishment of certain facts to which certain values are indissolubly attached, then it is relatively easy to see how the distinction between explicit purpose or over-all policy-making and the execution of this over-all policy can be maintained. But we have also asserted not only that educational administrators accept explicit purposes, but also that they do not modify these purposes by "administering," although they may be responsible for detecting changes in purpose and, at times, for devising the mechanisms for registering such changes. Furthermore, we have extended this theory to all organizations, except those in which the administrator is also the owner or an entrepreneur. Even then he is limited in his power to adopt or modify organizational purposes by the value system of society at large.

As a step toward the testing of this assertion, we propose a design for a research project. First, a series of concrete proposals of what a given school system should accomplish may be as-

[6] Herbert A. Simon, *Administrative Behavior* (New York: The Macmillan Company, 1955), p. 197.

sembled. Some of the purposes and objectives will be immediate and verifiable; for example, the schools should teach children how to do long division. Others are more remote and intangible; for example, the schools should teach international good will. Now, from the point of view of purposes, none of these objectives is existent or present, although presumably they are possibilities; the children who are to be taught do not now possess these abilities, but it is presumed that they are capable of doing so. To these possibilities certain values adhere, which in contradistinction to the possibilities themselves are present and continuing. The ability to do long division is desirable both now and when the children learn how to do it. The fact that it is a means to even further ends need not concern us at this time, since it is an objective of the school organization. Within the framework of present and continuing values and the objectives to which, when they are attained the same values are attached, the administrator makes his decisions.

The objection may be raised here that in the accomplishment of purposes or objectives, methods are adopted that possess intrinsic value, and that in some degree the "going is the goal." The decision about whether to adopt one method over another because it possesses greater intrinsic and immediate values would seem to introduce additional objectives. If method A will teach Johnny long division but involves undesirable side effects, then it is true that a school principal may adopt method B, which is less effective, but also less tedious, odious, or painful. But what has actually happened is that for the simple end in view of learning how to do long division a more complicated set of objectives has been substituted. The objectives now are that Johnny shall learn long division insofar as this is possible without making him bored or unhappy up to a certain point. So the means are adopted with both ends in view. The lack of clarity here seems to arise in part at least from the absence of a clear statement of the objectives of the schools.

After these statements of purposes have been assembled, the next step would be to collect samples of administrative decisions, which, when recorded, should be carefully analyzed and classified into two categories: first, those decisions or components of decisions that are made ostensibly to adopt means for the accomplishment of stated and implied objectives; and, second, those that are made ostensibly to change objectives, either directly, or indirectly by the adoption of means that would reasonably be expected to do so. Such analysis would require technical distinctions between fact and value components. In both categories the decisions would include an element that is theoretically warrantable at some time in the future by empirical facts; and in the first category, they would, except for irrelevant value choices, include only this element, since they are made in accord with accepted purposes. In the second, they would include *de novo* value decisions, either explicit or implicit, that would modify the accepted purposes. If our theory is correct, there will be few decisions in the second category.

The emergence of a full-time administrative class in educational organizations, which we assume is performing the duties we have specified, has been accounted for in this theory by the increase in the number, complexity, and urgency of the activities performed within the organization. At this stage in the development of the study of administration, general historical studies of the growth of administration in educational and other types of organizations should be undertaken.[7] Also, a series of specific statistical investigations could be designed to show how administrative duties increase in proportion to the number, distribution, complexity, and urgency of the activities carried on within organizations. It is surprising that more research to test has not been done on this frequently cited problem. The effect of administration on the complexity of organization and in turn on its growth is also worthy of investigation; and certainly Parkinson's law [8] may provide a serious hypothesis for research.

[7] See Frederick W. Terrien and Donald W. Mills, "The Effect of Changing Size upon the Internal Structure of Organizations," *American Sociological Review*, xx (1955).

[8] C. Northcote Parkinson, *Parkinson's Law* (Boston: Houghton-Mifflin Company, 1957).

That the co-ordinating aspect of administration requires a specific structure, commonly referred to as line and staff, as well as certain identifiable personal qualities in administrators constitutes a series of assumptions that are difficult to verify. The first students of administration identified a line structure in organizations that they deemed necessary to the administrative function. More recently, students of educational administration have assumed that the educational organization had merely imitated industrial and military administration, and that more appropriate and "democratic" structures not only could be devised but also would be more effective. An analysis of the administrative processes in educational organizations that have allegedly abandoned the line-and-staff structure might reveal whether or not they actually have done so and, if they have, the consequences that have resulted. Such an analysis, however, would be extremely difficult to do, since the essential process could easily be camouflaged with euphemistic descriptions. Perhaps, an analysis of the language used to describe the new structure would reveal whether or not the line principle has been abandoned. Also, through the method of participant observation,[9] substitute structures for the line organization may be observed and analyzed to determine to what extent they actually vary from the original pattern.

As for the personal qualities that are related to administrative success, the psychology of personality and of group behavior should be able to provide the means for testing our assumptions. Some of the current interest in the investigation of the phenomena of groups might be deflected to study the effect of personality traits on group behavior in formal organizations. Such traits as we have called "prevoyance" and "generalism" can undoubtedly be defined in such a way that they may be correlated with evidences of administrative success.

To attempt to confirm our theory of the social role of edu-

[9] For an excellent discussion of this method, see Howard S. Becker, "Problems of Inference and Proof in Participant Observation," *American Sociological Review*, XXIII, No. 6 (December, 1958), 653–60.

cational administration, and of administration in general, would be an extremely ambitious undertaking. Although pronouncements are made daily about the concomitant effects, both personal and social, of the growth of administration and its attendant bureaucracy, systematic studies are difficult to do. Long-range historical and comparative studies of social orders might show the effects of the growth of administration. Also more limited sociological analyses of communities could reveal the role that administration plays in maintaining an equilibrium of organizational life through its public relations function. And as for the spread of bureaucratic effects, systematic studies of the "organization man" in his behavior outside his organization might be revealing.

The final major proposition of this general theory, and one that may also be very controversial, is that the administrative process as we have defined it and as it is demanded by organization is incompatible with some aspects of education; that, in effect, the institutionalization of education which is necessary because of the complexity of the task has in turn created conditions that interfere with the educational process. Studies can be devised to show the effects of hierarchical organization and bureaucratic routines on creative work and on individuals capable of creative work who are dependent on organizations.

This list of possibilities for research is suggestive rather than exhaustive. Perceptive students who are research-minded will be able unquestionably to deduce many hypotheses other than the ones suggested here that are amenable to some form of verification. In line with our liberal and catholic views about the nature and importance of theory, it should be kept in mind at this stage in the study of educational administration that research does not have to be of the standard "scientific method" variety that attempts in every instance to establish a relationship. Observation, definition, and classification can all make important contributions to the advancement of the discipline, as can logical analysis, historical research in the sense of recreating the past, and careful comparative studies. While some of the techniques may be crude and yield only rather gross results, they may be refined through use. And the gross results can be of the utmost significance.

Implications for Practice

This general theory of administration is not designed to aid practice directly. Rather, it purports to provide a conceptual framework, a set of mutually consistent propositions, and a number of assertions about relationships that should provide a source of ideas and hypotheses. It is a fallacy common to many works on administrative theory that they should provide a program for practice.[10] However, since this theory assumes that administration is emerging as the kind of enterprise described, those aspects of it that withstand logical and empirical tests will have extraordinary influence on practice.

The first assumption, that administration is *sui generis* and common to all organizations, would indicate that administrators are interchangeable. If this assumption is true, administrators in industry, government, and education could perform equally well in almost any organization as long as they are not required to engage in the intrinsic functions of the organizations. Some evidence that this assumption is in accord with practice is found in institutions of higher learning. Keith Funston moved from the presidency of a small liberal arts college to that of the New York Stock Exchange, and Arthur Flemming has been a director of personnel in government and a college president, as well as a Secretary in the President's Cabinet. To be sure, public school systems have not adopted this practice, but there is no evidence that it would not be feasible if it were given a fair trial. This is not to say that

[10] See, for example, Roald Campbell and T. Gregg, *Administrative Behavior in Education* (New York: Harper & Brothers, 1957), Part III.

Implications for Research and Practice

there are no personal attachments or preferences due to temperament or background that could not cause an administrator to be happier or to feel more at home in one organization or another. It is often fashionable for administrators in educational organizations to lament the fact that the burden of administrative duties prevents their engaging in teaching, research, or other scholarly activities. But there seems to be no evidence that nostalgia for the life of a teacher or a scholar contributes to administrative success.

If our theory of the nature of the administrative task is valid, it will effect an extraordinary change in the practices of selecting and training administrators. Preparation for administration in general, with some regard for the intrinsic functions of the organization, because of their intimate relations with the administrative function, would supplant the prolonged training of "educators." Methods of discerning the purposes of education, coordination, and public relations would provide the three major foci for training. No recommendation is made here that new practices be adopted until either by systematic study or trends in practice our theory has more conclusive verification. However, some of its practical implications can be anticipated.

Varied and vague solutions are frequently recommended for the alleged incompatibility between administration and certain aspects of education. One of the most frequent is the recommendation that the educational administrator strive to remain a professional educator; that is, that he place educational necessities before those of the organization. However desirable this solution may be, we believe that it is practically impossible, since the very nature of the administrative task demands that the administrator heed the demands of the organization, *qua* organization. Another solution, which recognizes that the size and complexity of organizations are responsible for the increase and importance of the administrative function, proposes the decentralization of education into small, autonomous organizations. Again, there is the question of how practicable this proposal is. In addition to the trend, whatever the causes, toward larger administrative units, it is generally recognized that educational organizations must attain considerable size in order to provide the means and the variety of intrinsic functions necessary to accomplish their objectives. For example, in public education a discrepancy between the responsibility of an organization to provide adequate facilities and the sources of fiscal support has brought on the recommendation for larger school districts.

Notwithstanding the necessity of administration and its attendant bureaucracy—or perhaps because of it—concern about its relation to the technical, creative, and professional functions of an organization is apparently becoming more serious. Admiral Rickover, whose perception of this problem may be neurotically clear because of some of his experiences in government organization, has said:

> Somehow every organization must make room for innerdirected, obstreperous, creative people; sworn enemies of routine and the *status quo*, always ready to upset the applecart by thinking up new and better ways of doing things. They are the troublesome mavericks, unloved by the administrator who cannot forgive their contempt for conventions.[11]

He does not, however, suggest how this may be done. If our assumption is correct that by their very natures administration and some aspects of the educative process are incompatible, and that both must be contained in one organization, then the solution to the problem must be worked out on somewhat mechanical lines. In conclusion, we submit a tentative solution, which, although far from original and probably in extended use, is not often recognized or accepted.

Since it appears that many aspects of the educational function of organizations suffer little or none by conforming to administrative demands, and may indeed be facilitated by them, it is recommended that these aspects bear the burden of administra-

[11] H. G. Rickover, *Education and Freedom* (New York: E. P. Dutton and Company, 1959), p. 22.

tion. First, all housekeeping and bookkeeping activities should be performed in a routine fashion and largely by people for whom routine is not uncongenial. If the administrative virtues such as regularity, promptness, and accuracy are demonstrated in the handling of these matters, the stability of the organization will be enhanced. Much of the education itself may also be routinized: drill or practice, demonstrations, explanation and exposition, some lectures, translations, and examinations can all be scheduled with no obvious interference with the activities themselves. Careful and rigid co-ordination of these activities may not only maintain the organization, but it may also give it enough stability to allow a great deal of freedom in the pursuit of nonroutine activities if the distinction between the two is recognized. The organizational demands must be met—every classroom must have a teacher who is not assigned elsewhere at the same time—but once the demands are met, the temptation to subject all additional activities to them should be avoided.

On the second hand, educational organizations may employ appropriate personnel and otherwise provide for those aspects of education that seem to conflict with administrative routines. At the college and university level the artist in residence, the professor at large, and the independent researcher may pursue their own intellectual and creative interests; and this procedure has been adapted to the lower schools in the resource teachers, who with comparatively free schedules may work with students as well as teachers. Even the same personnel who have the routine schedules to bear may be given free periods to engage in unscheduled activities.

Another distinction that might be made is that between administrative and substantive co-ordination. It is administratively necessary to assign so many classes to a geometry teacher, to assign him a room, and a time schedule. It is not administratively necessary ordinarily to assign him a methodology of teaching that corresponds to that used by every geometry teacher in the school. Freedom of method, particularly with intelligent, experienced, and educated teachers, would lift an unnecessary administrative burden from the educative process and allow for greater originality, imagination, and creativity. From what we know about the comparative efficiency of different methods, administrators may feel free to adopt such procedures.

This same general principle, that of allowing certain aspects of education to carry the administrative burden of the organization, can also be applied to the public relations function. Some of the intrinsic activities of an educational organization may be easily supported, easily "sold" because the objectives to which they are directed are urgent, immediate, or obviously utilitarian; other activities equally, or perhaps more, important ultimately for the attainment of organizational purposes are much more difficult and sometimes virtually impossible to support. Therefore, the administrative device of obtaining excess funds for those activities that are supportable and diverting the excess to the support of less "salable" activities is defensible; and certainly it is practiced. An extreme example is the financing of esoteric academic functions through the gate receipts from football, which more than pays for itself. Other practices include diverting the profits, or to use the more euphemistic term "overhead," from service activities, evening schools, and contract research to carry some of the less supportable activities of a university. And in public education funds may be obtained for vocational or social education that may indirectly be used to support the less obviously practical educational pursuits.

Frank recognition of this necessity, if it is a necessity, may relieve the uneasiness administrators have about the ethics of this kind of distribution of the support that accrues to an organization through their efforts. And it may prevent their adopting the practice of supporting only those educational activities for which they are able to obtain outside support, thereby discouraging other activities that in the long run may contribute more to the accomplishment of an organization's purposes than those that are easily supported. Although all the ends of an organization may be

Implications for Research and Practice

willed, it does not follow that sufficient means for all are. The administrative task has the responsibility for making the means correspond to the ends, not only in solicitation but also in distribution. And so we have returned to the administrative necessity for knowing the purposes of an organization and the order of their importance.

Index

Adams, Brooks, 12, 32–33, 111
Administration, educational: science of, 5, 7, 22, 27; definition, 9–13, 37–41 *passim*, 56–57, 63, 186–88; functions of, 27, 36, 41–42, 61, 63, 148; growth of, 31–32, 35, 36, 56–57, 91, 145, 191, 193, 195; organization of, 34, 47–49; social role of, 35–36, 131–32, 137–49; and public relations, 36, 41; and policy formation, 41, 44–52, 108–09, 126; in transitional stage, 57; and decisions, 80; history of, 91; nature of, 145; compared to teaching, 170; preparation for, 195. *See also* Administration, educational, literature; Administration, educational, theory of; Administration, *sui generis*; Administration's conflict with education; Administrative elite; Co-ordination; Line and staff organization; "Managerial revolution;" Organizations; Policy formation; Public relations; Purpose, discernment of

Administration, educational, literature: lack of, 5, 61, 123; review of, 23–33

Administration, educational, theory of: lack of, 5, 29, 30; new interest and study of, 7, 16, 18, 22, 29–31; value for administration, 20; aspects of, 22–23, 33–34; history of, 23–29; review of literature, 23–33; evaluation, 184–94, 195

Administration, *sui generis*, 26–27, 30–35 *passim*, 57, 141, 150, 186, 188, 194–96

Administration's conflict with education, 167, 168–83, 193, 195–98; proposition, 170–71; in discernment of purpose, 171–73; in co-ordination, 173–78; in public relations, 178–79; in values, 179–80

Administrative decisions. *See* Decisions, administrative

Administrative elite, 35, 191. *See also* "Managerial revolution"

Administrators, educational: and theory, 20; dual role of, 24, 43, 47,

201

Administrators, educational (cont.)
57–60, 147, 169–70; and purposes of education, 27, 36; criteria for, 36, 60, 72, 78, 83, 173, 180, 182, 192, 195; and purposes of organization, 41–42, 50, 53, 57–58; as teachers, 47, 57; nature of role, 47, 50–52, 57–58, 60–61, 71–72, 188, 195; and administrative decisions, 52–54; future role, 56–58; compared to other administrators, 58, 60–61; in literature, 61; and policy formation, 71–73, 127–29, 136, 147–48; exceptions to role, 72–76; and special interest groups, 72, 74–75; range of opportunities for, 125–26; and public relations, 127–29, 136. See also Administration, educational; Administrative elite; Decisions, administrative; Education, purposes of; Policy formation; Public relations; Purpose, discernment of
Advanced Research Project Agency, 60
A. E. (George Russell), 111
Alberty, Harold, 152–53
Allocating, 90, 102–03. See also Coordination
American Association of School Administrators, 89
Analysis. See Theory
Aristotle, 20
Art Students League, 171
Ashmore, Henry, 68–69
Austin, Texas, school personnel roster, 91
Authority: definition, 104; in co-ordination, 104–08; in democratic society, 104–07, 115; sources, 106–15. See also "Charisma;" Coordination; Fairness; "Generalism:" Leadership

Babbitt, Irving, 38–39
Barnard, Chester I., 124

Benne, Kenneth D., 105
Bernays, Edward L., 120–21; *The Engineering of Consent*, 121
Betjeman, John, 123–24
Blackwell, Gordon W., 130–31
Boards of education, 140–42 *passim*; dual role of, 70, 88; and administration, 72–73; and special interest groups, 74; and policy formation, 79, 122, 138, 172; and co-ordination, 106. See also Boards of education, local; Boards of education, state
Boards of education, local: and policy formation, 64, 67–70, 74; dual role of, 67–70
Boards of education, state: and policy formation, 64, 67, 70, 74; source of authority, 66; authority, 66; dual role of, 74
Boring, Edwin G., 8
Brahe, Tycho, 7
Bridgman, P. W., 10, 11
British colonial officials, 112
Buermeyer, Laurence, 184
Buffalo, New York, 147
Bureaucracy, 182–83, 193, 196; growth of, 145–48, 169–70; criteria for, 146; and democratic values, 146–47, 148. See also Administration, educational; Organizations
Burnham, James, 33

Caesar, Julius, 98
Carnegie, Dale, 133
Carnegie unit, 175
"Charisma," 114–15. See also Authority
Chase, Francis S., 14
Chicago, University of (Illinois), 75
Chief Justice of the Supreme Court, 59–60
Citizens' Committee, 84–85. See also "Community will"
Clark, Burton R., 125
Classification. See Theory

Coladarci, Arthur P., 12–13, 29
College presidents, 188; ambiguous role as administrator, 72, 75–76
Colorado School of Mines, 151
Community survey, 84. See also "Community will"
"Community will," 71, 78, 80, 81–85, 120–22 passim, 132, 139–41, 148; in policy formation, 70–72, 78, 80, 81–85, 138, 147; definition, 81–82, 139; and democratic values, 141. See also Education, public support for; Public relations
Congress, U. S., 126
"Consideration," 111
Constitutions: state, 64–70 passim; federal, 64–65, 70; and policy formation, 64, 79, 122, 138; and co-ordination, 106. See also Tenth amendment
Continental Congress, 70
Cooperative Program in Educational Administration, 28–29
Co-ordination, 42, 63, 86–117, 118, 187, 195, 197; definition, 87, 88–90; functions of, 88; origin, 90–93; growth of, 91; and democratic values, 93–95, 97, 100, 104–07, 115, 192; necessary conditions for, 95–108; structure of, 95–104; authority for, 104–08; limitations of, 115–17; conflict with education, 173–78. See also Administration, educational, functions of; Allocating; Authority; Directing; Staffing
Courts: state, 64; federal, 64, 70; and policy formation, 70, 79, 80, 138, 172; and co-ordination, 106
"Creative teaching," 177
Cubberley, Ellwood P., 23–24

Dahl, Robert A., 31, 52
Dampier-Whetham, W. C. D., 6–7
Decisions, administrative: definition—distinguished from decisions of purpose, 44–52; warranting of, 52–56; element of purpose, 53–54; element of means, 54–55; element of choice, 55; sources of authority for, 80; discretion in, 179; evaluation, 180–81. See also Administration, educational; Administrators, educational
Decisions of means, 55. See also Decisions, administrative
Decisions of purpose, 55. See also Decisions, administrative
Definition: problem of, 37–44; lexical, 38–40, 186; evaluation, 186–87. See also Theory
DeGarmo, Charles, 162–63; Aesthetic Education, 162
Democratic values. See Authority; Bureaucracy; Co-ordination
de Tocqueville, Alexis, 107
Dewey, John, 152, 155, 156, 164; Democracy and Education, 155
Directing, 90. See also Co-ordination
Direction of activities. See Co-ordination
Discernment of purpose. See Purpose, discernment of
"double interchange," 159
Ducasse, C. J., 15n

Education: science of, 27; and administration, 27, 36; purposes of, 51, 135, 189–90; confusion of purposes, 52, 77; nature of, 79, 150–67; source of authority for, 102; social role, 137–49, 192, 193; theories of, 152; paradoxes of, 154–56. See also Social needs
Education, conflict with administration. See Administration's conflict with education
Education, public support for, 118, 157, 178–79, 187–88, 196, 198. See also "Community will;" Legislatures; Public relations
Educational administration. See Administration, educational

Educational administrators. *See* Administrators, educational
Edwards, Newton D., 65
Eliot, Charles William, 75
Empiricism. *See* Theory
Ennius, 157
Explanation. *See* Theory

Fairness, 113. *See also* Authority
Fayol, Henri, 2, 14, 26–35 *passim*, 40, 87
Federal Bureau of Investigation, 126–27
Feigl, Herbert, 17
Flemming, Arthur, 194
Forster, Charles R., 61
Fowler, Henry Watson, 39
Friedrich, Carl Joachim, 45–46
Funston, Keith, 194

Gary, Indiana, The Public School System of, 69, 73
Gaus, John M., 31
"Generalism," 111–13, 192. *See also* Authority
Getzels, Jacob W., 12–13, 29
Gibb, Cecil A., 110
Gilman, Daniel Coit, 75
Graicunas, V. A., 92
Groton, 151
Guetzkow, Harold, 112
Gulick, Luther H., 2, 12, 14, 26–35 *passim*, 40, 117

Hagman, Harlan L., 14, 28
Hall, Roy M., 101
Halpin, Andrew W., 14, 94, 110–11
Harper, William Rainey, 75
Harris, William Torrey, 34
Harvard University, 75
Hayek, Friedrich A., 145
Hobson, Robert L., 113
Holzman, P. S., 112
Hooker, Richard, 128
Horace, 154; *Carpe Diem*, 154

Hull, Clark L., 17–18
Hunt, Holman, 161
Huxley, Thomas, 152
Hypothetico-deductive theory. *See* Theory

Identification. *See* Theory
"Imitation" hypothesis, 95
"Informing" activities, 127. *See also* Public relations
"Initiating Structure-in-Interaction," 111
"Interactional theory," 110
International Correspondence Schools, 151

Jefferson, Thomas, 158
Johns Hopkins University, The, 75
Judiciary Act of 1789, 70

Kafka, Franz, 168
Kepler, Johannes, 7
Klein, G. S., 112

Langfitt, R. Emerson, 174
Lamb, Charles, 153
Leadership, 108–11. *See also* Authority
Leathers, Frank P., 101
Legislatures: federal, 64, 79, 122, 138; and policy formation, 64, 79, 122, 138, 141–42, 172; state, 66, 67, 70, 127; and special interest groups, 74; ambiguities of, 79–80; and co-ordination, 106; and administration, 126; support for education, 130. *See also* Policy formation
Lewis, Clarence Irving, 156
Leys, Wayne A. R., 71
Lindsay, R. B., 9
Line and staff organization, 34, 95–102, 103, 192; description, 97–99; and democratic values, 97, 100, 115; schematic diagram, 99; at-

Index

tempts to abolish, 99–101. See also Co-ordination; Staffing
Lippmann, Walter, 77
Liverpool, England, 132
Lobbying, 133. See also Public relations
Louisville, Kentucky, 147
Lowes, John Livingstone, 165–66
Lucretius, 157

McDougall, William, 81
Magnay, H. S., 132
Maier, N. R. F., 112
"Managerial revolution," 145, 147, 191; in education, 34–35
Mann, Horace, 43
Marx, Fritz Morstein, 145
Maryland: constitution, 65–66; State Board of Education, 66; public school laws, 66–67, 72–73
Merton, Robert K., 23
Metatheory, 2, 5. See also Theory
Millay, Edna St. Vincent, 185
Moehlmann, Arthur B., 119, 120
Mooney, James D., 87
Mort, Paul R., 24–26
Moses, 20
Murray, Arthur, Dance Studio, 151

National Defense Education Act, 70
Naval Academy, U. S., 151
Nazis, 158
New Deal, 126
Newlon, Jesse H., 24
Newman, John Cardinal, 156
Newton, Sir Isaac, 17; *Principia*, 17
New York Stock Exchange, 194
Niebuhr, Reinhold, 105–06

Observation. See Theory
Ohio, revenue structure, 130
"Organization man," 50, 61, 148, 193
Organizations: purposes of, 41–42, 53; educational, 47; nature of, 48–49, 128, 150; within organizations, 72, 73–74; definition and structure, 86–87; growth of, 86, 91, 119, 142; complexity of, 91–93; failure of, 124–25; competition between, 129–33, 143; as tool of education, 176. See also Administration, educational; Administrators, educational; Bureaucracy

Parent Teacher Association, 122
Parker, DeWitt H., 162
Parkinson's law, 93, 191
Parsons, Talcott, 150, 159
"Pathetic fallacy," 94
Pennsylvania, state laws, 67
Pittenger, Benjamin Floyd, 12, 96–97, 102
Planned society, 129–33, 144
Plato, 152, 155; *Republic*, 155
Policy formation, 189–91; and administration, 34, 44–52, 56, 79, 80–81, 127, 136, 186–87; definition, 44–45; agencies for, 49, 51–52, 63–85 *passim*, 122, 125, 138, 147, 171, 172; method of determination, 63–78; in private education, 67; centralization of, 162; use of public relations in, 127, 129, 136. See also Administration, educational; Administrators, educational; Boards of education; Constitutions; Courts; Legislatures
Popular will. See "Community will"
POSDCORB, 14
Private education, 69, 121, 139; policy formation in, 67; competition in, 129
"Procedural" co-ordination, 116. See also Co-ordination
"Professionals" in education, 170
Public opinion poll, 84. See also "Community will"
Public relations, 41, 42, 58, 63, 83, 109, 118–36, 178–79, 187–88,

Public relations (continued) 193, 195, 198; justification of, 118–19, 129; definition, 119–23, 129, 178; legitimacy of, 123–29; abuse of, 127–29; and social planning, 129–33; responsibility for, 133–34; rules for practice, 133, 134–36; conflict with education, 178–79. See also Administration, educational, functions of; Administrators, educational; "Community will;" Education, public support for; Policy formation
Public School System of Gary, Indiana, The, 69, 73
Public support. See Education, public support for
Public will. See "Community will"
Purdue University studies
Purpose, discernment of, 44, 63–85, 109, 118, 120, 126, 127, 137–42 passim, 187–91 passim, 195, 199; changes in, 64, 79; and administrative role, 71–72; exceptions, 72–76; methods for, 78–85; variety and difficulty of, 78, 80, 152; conflict with education, 171–73. See also Administration, educational, functions of; Administrators, educational

Reiley, Alan C., 87
Rembrandt van Rijn, 161
Rickover, Hyman G., 196
River Rouge plant (Detroit, Michigan), 131
Roberts, Charles T., 101
Roman Catholic Church, 102, 124
Rousseau, Jean Jacques, 139
Royal Institution, 152
Royce, Josiah, 81

St. Ignatius, 152
St. Johns College (Annapolis, Maryland), 151

Schopenhauer, Arthur, 54
Schwartz, Alfred, 14, 28
Sears, Jesse B., 2, 12, 14, 26–28, 34, 35
Second International Congress of Administrative Science (Brussels, Belgium, 1923), 31
Shorey, Paul, 154–55
Simon, Herbert A., 11, 22, 49–50, 94, 116, 181, 189
Skogsberg, Alfred H., 95
Smithburg, Donald, 11, 94
"Social interpretation," 119, 121
Social needs, 138–43, 171, 172. See also Education, purposes of
Social role of administration. See Administration, social role of
"Social will." See "Community will"
Spears, Harold, 100
Special interest groups, 72, 74–75. See also Policy formation
Spencer, Herbert, 156
Staffing, 88–90, 102–03. See also Co-ordination; Line and staff organization
Stene, Edwin Otto, 34
Stephens, Leslie, 155
Stogdill, Ralph M., 109
Stoke, Harold W., 76
"Substantive" co-ordination, 116. See also Co-ordination
Supreme Court, U. S., 64, 70, 139; Chief Justice, 59–60

Taylor, Francis, 59
Taylor, Frederick W., 26
Teachers: and policy formation, 49, 51; as administrators, 60–61; in literature, 61; criteria for, 88–90, 133, 173, 180, 182; and public relations, 133, 134; role in society, 156. See also Teaching
Teaching, 47; public relations in, 133; nature of, 153n–55 passim, 163–

Index

66; compared to administration, 170. *See also* Teachers
Tead, Ordway, 92
Tenth amendment, 64. *See also* Constitutions, federal
Thames River, England, 152
Theory: etymology of, 6; types of, 6–18; observation, 6–7; identification, 7–9, 18; definition, 9–13, 20; classification, 13–14, 18, 20; analysis, 13–14, 20; empiricism, 14–15; explanation, 15n–17, 20; hypothetico-deductive, 17–19; range of, 18–20; applications of, 19; prestige of, 19–20; limitations of, 20; definition of, 184; evaluation of, 184–86; nature of, 193. *See also* Metatheory

Thompson, Victor A., 11, 94
Thorp, Margaret Farrand, 75
Tocqueville, Alexis de, 107
Tycho Brahe, 7

Urwick, L., 2, 12, 97–98

Weber, Max, 114, 145–46, 148, 169, 182
West, Rebecca, 168; "The Twentieth Century Bureaucrat," 168
Willoughby, W. F., 32
Wilson, Charles H., 58–59
Wilson, Woodrow, 30, 46
Wundt, Wilhelm Max, 81; *Volker Psychologie*, 81

Zeitgeist, 110